for
GIRLS
only

FRANK HOWARD RICHARDSON, M.D.

for GIRLS only

The Doctor Discusses
the
Mysteries of Womanhood

DAVID McKAY COMPANY, INC.

To think that you are teaching,
and find that you are being taught
To feel sure that you are right,
and then realize that you are wrong
To have your ideal of what a daughter ought to be
brushed aside, while a reality that is better
takes its place—
These are some of the experiences
of a Dad growing up

And so
This little volume is gratefully dedicated to
MARY AND RUTH

FOREWORD

◻

By Amos Christie, M.D.

Professor of Pediatrics, Vanderbilt University School of Medicine, Nashville, Tennessee

Although there is nothing in these pages to indicate it, Doctor Richardson has written this book for Mrs. Christie and for me. So far as we are concerned, the fact that its title says it was written for teen-age girls only is purely coincidental. How dearly we love ours; and how very much we would like to understand her and to have her understand us.

You see, I am a professor of pediatrics. I know a great deal about the physical growth and development of the young; but I must say, with Ogden Nash, "Oh Adolescence, Oh Adolescence, I wince before thine incandescence." I am constantly impressed by the concern my adolescent patients show regarding matters of health, figure or body build, and their anxieties about many other things.

Some of these things they cannot verbalize; others they just feel in uncomfortable, unconscious ways. What we pediatricians, psychologists, clergymen and teachers need to know is what these things are all about, and what we ought to do about them.

Doctor Richardson, himself a father and a physician, refutes in this little volume the old adage of the Chinese philosopher, "He who knows, does not tell; he who tells, does not know." He knows, from wide personal experience, and he tells all—or almost all. In an easy conversational style he has a wise camp director and a woman medical advisor tell our daughters and their parents how these daughters are trying to establish and maintain positions of independence for themselves. He shows how they attempt to break away from security and protection, insisting on the rights and privileges of the adult without as yet being able to stand on their own feet.

We parents and teachers continually add to their frustration by expecting adult performance in conduct and behavior from ones who matured physiologically only last year. To understand these things is a big order. Yet we parents have gone this far, and will never be satisfied until we have tried to go the whole distance in order to help our daughters mature emotionally as well as physically.

Doctor Richardson has helped our home by this volume. I believe the contents of this book will help others to understand their daughters, and their daughters to understand them. In other words, the title is misleading; for it is written every bit as much for parents as for their daughters.

This little book shows in a number of ways how good mental health begins at home; and how this good mental health, in parents and other adults surrounding these adolescent girls, can bring about the security and affectionate know-how that must be the basis for sound, mature and stable family relationships.

AMOS CHRISTIE

Nashville, Tennessee

CONTENTS

◻

CONTENTS

INTRODUCTION

◻

By KATHARINE F. LENROOT

Former Chief, Children's Bureau, United States Government

WRITTEN WITH A WEALTH OF UNDERSTANDING, THIS little book should bring enlightenment and inspiration to many who are crossing the threshold between childhood and young girlhood and to adults lovingly concerned with problems at this crucial stage. An atmosphere of simple, everyday experience centered in life at a girls' camp is created by the author, a wise doctor with years of experience in keeping children well. In him, scientific knowledge is combined with the art of human relations; he has entered into the lives of daughters and their mothers through all stages of infancy, childhood, and youth.

The *dramatis personae* in this story of absorbing interest are the girls, their mothers, the director of a girls' camp, and a woman physician with a lively interest in youth. Backstage are the boys, who often seem to the girls mysterious, a little troublesome, and yet persons whose attention and liking are greatly to be desired.

The treatment of the themes dealt with is based on the concept that at each stage in the process of growing up there are problems to be solved and that success in their solution prepares the way for further growth. Although bodily changes are important, it is their impact on one's understanding of one's self and what one wants to be like and to become, and on one's relationships with others, that constitutes the central meaning of adolescence.

Among the questions which the camp director and the doctor help the girls to answer are those concerning a new baby expected in the home of one of the girls; why a girl both loves and rebels against her mother; friendships with other girls and with boys; petting; how to be popular; the tragic experience of having a baby out of wedlock, the importance of preparing for happy married life.

Mothers, teachers, camp counsellors, and all who work with girls, as well as the girls themselves, for whom and to whom the book is written, will be inspired by the simplicity of the treatment and the ideals that are evident on every page.

"We learned," the camp director tells the girls at the last campfire, "that we all go through a number of emotional stages. Each stage is important; and we take along with us through life some of the characteristics of each period of development. But there is always a danger that somewhere along the line between babyhood and womanhood we might stop, and stay too long at one stage. . . . If you know these things, you can help yourselves to grow up."

That is just what this little book offers to its young readers—help in understanding themselves and, on the basis of that understanding, help in living life at each stage with zest, with humor, and with a developing insight into the needs and problems of others. On such a foundation can be built strength and compassion for all of life's journey.

KATHARINE F. LENROOT

Hartsdale, New York

WHAT DO GIRLS TALK ABOUT?

□ □ □ □ □ □ □ □ □ □ □ □

"MARY ANN JUST MAKES ME SICK THE WAY SHE FLOUNCES around at school as if she owned the universe."

"Yes, she gives me a pain, too. I can't stand the way she fixes her hair, as if she were sixteen years old. She's big enough to be twenty, but she's only fourteen. And have you noticed the lipstick she puts on? My mother would have a fit if I ever looked like that. I have to buy my lipstick without her knowing it, and put it on at school."

The two girls, Helen and Nell, had been sitting at a table in the corner drug store, sipping a soft drink from a bottle. They had started to get up, when who should walk in but Mary Ann and Jack. The girls instantly sat back in their chairs, played with their bottles, and pretended to look the other way.

"Speaking of angels," Helen whispered.

"Or should I say devils?" Nell muttered.

"Doesn't she think she is wonderful having a date? She acts as if she owned him, but I saw Jack yesterday with Betty and the day before with Jane. Mary Ann needn't act as if she were the only one."

Mary Ann and Jack sat at the counter. Each ordered a soda bulging with ice cream, completely ignoring Helen and Nell. The girls had seen enough; so they decided it was time to go: but as Helen passed behind them she could not resist the temptation of catching her foot, which was none too dainty, in Mary Ann's stool, almost knocking her over.

When out on the street of their little town, they decided to go to the post office and pick up the mail and then walk by the ball field and watch their team practice. There was almost a feeling of summer in the air. It was time to be thinking about going to camp soon. Both girls had gone the previous year, and were planning to return. Mary Ann was going also, but for the first time. They still could not get her out of their minds. Somehow she had gotten under their skin.

"Well, I know one thing. When Mary Ann gets to camp, she's going to have some of that stuck-up air knocked out of her. I can hardly wait for a swimming meet or tennis match. I *know* I can beat her all to pieces."

Helen added: "Yes, and I bet she doesn't know how to handle a canoe either. Then she will not be holding her nose in the air as if she were so much better than we are. And there will be no boys there, either, for her to try to show off before. I can hardly wait for camp to open. By the way, did you know that Lady is going to speak before the Woman's Club sometime this summer? She is going to tell our mothers all about everything, what the camp stands for, what we do and"—

"And," added Nell with a laugh, "what our mothers are *not* to send us—a big box of candy or an enormous cake. Will you ever forget when Betty was sent all those goodies from home? Lady would not let her have them, but made her divide them all at dinner time. But do you know, she was a good sport about it. Anyhow, just to look at Lady makes you want to do the right thing. She is so wonderful; and isn't she beautiful?"

"I can see her now in that gorgeous blue dress, the night of the banquet. I wish I could be just like her when I grow up."

As they were approaching the ball field, a car honked and stopped. It was Helen's mother.

"Girls, don't you want to hop in and go for a ride? I have some marketing to do; and if you like, you can choose what you want for supper. If it's sausage and pancakes, you may take over as cooks. I'll telephone Mrs. Brower, and I am sure she will let Nell stay for supper. We might ask Jane and Mary Ann too," but in unison both girls put thumbs down on Mary Ann. Mrs. Brown wisely did not ask for the reasons they did not want their old friend, with whom they had played since the first grade.

The three girls prepared the supper. As a surprise for Mr. and Mrs. Brown, they had bought a few extras in the way of nuts, also a package of marshmallows to toast in front of the open fire.

And so, with the dishes washed, the girls squatted in front of the fireplace with their long forks. Mrs. Brown had left the room; so they felt as free to talk as if they were at school. But she was in the next room, and she could hear pretty well what was going on. She heard Helen say:

"Oh, I wish school were not going to close quite yet. I just hate to think that I won't see Miss Cooper again for all summer. I did not expect to like algebra; but I studied my head off, just to have her give me one of her smiles."

"I wonder why she never married," added Jane. "You know she's old. She's twenty-four! I'm *sure* she must have had several love affairs. I bet she was engaged to be married, and he was killed in the war. I certainly expect to get married before I'm *that* old! I'm going to have eight children, and live in a great big house."

"I'm *never* going to get married," said Nell. "I don't like boys. I don't care if I'm never invited to a ball game. I am going to be like Florence Nightingale, and do something worth while in life."

"And don't you think it's worth while to get married and have lots of children?"

"Well, maybe, but I just don't want to."

"I hope you won't be like that awful Miss Miller, 'whose hair droops round her pallid cheeks like seaweed on a clam.'" They all laughed loudly.

"You wait and see. You'll change your tune when you start having dates and fun with the boys."

"And what do you call 'fun'? Having a boy hold your hand and kiss you? My mother said it was wicked to allow a boy even to touch you. She told me about Edna who had to leave school because she let a boy touch her."

"What about Edna? I knew she had to leave school; but what was it all about?"

"Why, didn't you know she was going to have a baby?"

In utter amazement both girls almost shrieked, "NO!"

"Tell us about it. I didn't know you *could* have a baby if you weren't married," said Jane. "What an awful thing! I knew that everything was 'hush, hush' about Edna; but I never dreamed such a thing could happen at high school. Rosemary ran off and got married. But Edna! she seemed so nice! I can't believe it; and I can't understand it, either."

"Well, she just let a boy kiss her, and that is what happened. My mother told me so."

"I just don't believe it," added Jane. "I'm going to ask Lady when I get to camp. She knows everything, and she knows Edna. She'll tell us all about it."

"Why don't you ask your mother to tell you?"

"Never! She would think I was awful even to think such thoughts. But I know one thing. Not every girl that holds hands with a boy and kisses him, has a baby. Look at all the girls at school who are doing it all of the time! You just *have* to be married first. I don't care what anybody says. I bet Edna ran off and got married, and nobody knew it.

"Did you see that book that one of the senior high school girls had? She answered an advertisement that said that if you wanted to know all about marriage, to send in a dollar and they would mail you a book in a plain envelope, so that no one would know what was in it. I just got a glimpse of it; but it was filled with all kinds of pictures. One of the teachers found it; and was she mad! She took it away, and said we had no business reading such things."

"I think we *ought* to have books like that," said Helen.

"The teacher must have read the book; for I heard her talking to another teacher at recess and she said that next year we were going to have a course on getting ready for marriage; that even at our age we ought to begin to think about it."

Mrs. Brown in the next room had heard the conversation that had gone on during the toasting of marshmallows. She was dumbfounded. She had not thought for one moment that "those children" could be talking like that. In fact she was horrified! But it had brought her to her senses, and she determined that something would have to be done about it. She felt relieved when Jane said,

"Give me one more marshmallow. The fire is going out and I must be going home. I still have a lot of things to do before I am ready for camp. Oh boy! won't it be fun." The girls stretched as they got up, a bit stiff from sitting so long. Mrs. Brown then came into the room, considerably wiser than when she went out.

"Well, girls, are you ready? Jump in the car and I'll take you home."

OFF TO CAMP

□ □ □ □ □ □ □ □ □ □ □ □

"NOW, LET'S GO OVER YOUR LIST CAREFULLY TO MAKE sure that nothing is omitted," said Jane's mother. "Don't forget you won't have too much room for your things when you get to camp. You're allowed an army locker at the foot of your bunk bed, and then there is a small closet for each girl. Don't you remember you had to send home about half of your clothes last year because you had no room for them? Well, I'll read out what you have on your list and you check: sheets, towels, soap, one heavy blanket, bathing suit."

"Yes, and just look at my bathing suit." Jane snatched it up and waved it in her mother's face. That had been the subject of many heartbreaking discussions; but Mrs. Clark had thought it had been settled, once and for all, that her last-year's bathing suit was good enough for another season. But no, once more she had to hear it all over again.

"Just look at this suit! You know blue is not my color. And the style of it belongs to the middle ages. They're just not wearing bathing suits this year with straps over the shoulders. You know everyone is going to laugh at me when I put it on. I just wish the moths had eaten it all up! I never have liked it."

.6.

"Well, dear, you are the one that picked it out last year."

"I don't care. You made me buy it."

"You thought it was pretty *then,* for you told me so."

"*Then* is not *now.* It is hideous, just hideous. But I suppose I'll have to take it," and she flung it into her trunk.

Her mother's heart sank into her shoes. She had hoped Jane's last day before leaving for camp would have been so happy, thinking of the fun she would have and getting ready for it.

Just then there was a banging at the door, and what looked like an army of girls burst into the room.

"Jane, Jane, the bus is going to be here an hour earlier than we thought! Why, aren't you packed yet? I was ready days ago. Hurry up, we'll help."

In a flash the locker was closed, the tennis racket put on top of it, and the accordion on top of that. The mother was ignored as they flew out of the door and down the street to rush into somebody else's house. It looked as if every girl in town were going to camp. They passed Mary Ann on the corner surrounded by a group of boys. Some of the girls tried to josh her a bit, but she showed that she felt very superior. The girls in the know laughed to themselves as they antici- pated what was going to happen to her when Lady once gave one of her talks.

Honk! honk! the camp bus swung round the corner and the girls all scampered, each to her own house, to stand ready by her belongings on the street so that no time would be lost in gathering every one up. The mothers were trying to give last minute words of advice to deaf ears, but when the bus stopped for each girl, her mother did generally get a big hug with, "Write me, Mom. Goodbye."

The bus was filled, and the girls shouted and yelled at everyone they saw as it rolled down the street and out of town. About half of the girls had been to camp the year before, but the other half were having this experience for the first time. If the truth were told, many of them were just a little frightened as they faced what to them was the unknown. Oh yes, they had heard a lot about everything, so as to know what to expect; and they had thought that they wanted to go to camp, but somehow waving goodbye to their mothers gave their hearts a tug they had not expected.

But soon the old timers were singing the camp songs, and the new girls found themselves joining in. There were two counselors on the bus, Kay and Fay. They were so nice, seniors at college. The old camp girls were crazy about them and knew their personal lives from A to Z, knew all about their love affairs. And Kay this year was wearing a diamond! It was going to be thrilling to hear all about him and when they were going to be married, what her wedding dress was going to look like, and all the parties she would be going to. And my, all the presents she would get! What fun to get married! most of them were thinking.

Kay and Fay were joining in the singing; but they also kept their eyes opened, and watched each girl carefully. Kay noticed one little girl sitting by the window. She was younger than the rest. She was looking out, and did not join in with the singing. Kay quietly got up out of her seat and went over to Bessie, asked the girl next to her to change seats, and slipped in and sat down. Kay did not know her, for she was a new girl.

"My, doesn't the country look beautiful," said Kay.

Bessie, without looking up, said, "Yes."

"And have you ever seen Lake Laughing Water?"

"No."

"And is this the first time you have ever been away from home?"

"Yes."

Still the girl looked out of the window. She evidently was not anticipating much fun in going to camp. It was up to Kay to win her, and to see that she had a good time. But something was evidently radically wrong. They both sat silent for a little while, then Kay began again:

"Have you any brothers or sisters?"

"Yes, a little brother."

"How old is he?"

"Six."

"Any more?"

Then Bessie's eyes filled up. She could hold in no longer.

"My mother is going to have a baby; and that's why they've sent me off to camp. They don't want me to be there when she dies."

"Dies! Why, she is not going to die!"

"Well, you know Mrs. Jones died when *she* had a baby."

"Oh, but she did not die because she had a baby. She had pneumonia at the time the baby was born. Why, to have a baby is nothing to be afraid of."

"Then why did they send me away?"

"Your mother wanted you to have a good time this summer, to get fat and rosy, and learn how to swim and play tennis. For don't you know, you are going to help with the baby when you get back home. There is so much you can do. You will be giving the baby his bath. They are so cunning, too tiny at first to do much kicking; but when they are a few months old, they will splash you all over."

Bessie's face brightened for the first time.

"This baby of yours is going to think you are the most wonderful mother's helper in the world. All the girls at school will envy you and want to come home from school to see him. You can roll the carriage while mother takes a nap or does the ironing. My, my, you will have to have bushels of fun at camp, eat big meals and get strong, to do all of those things."

"And you really don't think my mother is going to die?"

"Why, of course not. To have a baby is the most natural thing in the world. That is one reason why girls like myself want to get married and have a baby, and I certainly hope that I will. Do you think I would, if I thought I was going to die? When does your mother expect the baby?"

"I don't know; she didn't tell me. All I know is the cleaning woman said, 'Your mother is sure going to have a big baby. I know she'll have a hard time. I never saw anyone so large in all my days.' It scares me every time I think of it."

"Look here, when you get to camp Lady is going to tell you everything that you want to know. She'll tell us how babies are born, and that there is nothing to be afraid of. Dr. Marilyn Johnson, whom you'll just love, comes to camp several times; and the girls sit around the camp fire while they ask her questions. She tells us how our bodies work and how we are different from boys and why. She says that girls in high school can begin to think about how to live so that they too can be mothers that their children will be proud of, just as you are proud of your mother.

"Oh, there's the lake. We were so busy talking I had forgotten to look out of the window and notice where we are. In just a few minutes you'll see the cabins. Now remember, I'm going to be in camp all of the time; so that if there's anything that bothers you, or anything that you want to know, you come right to me. I must be getting back to my seat and pull down my barracks bag."

Bessie, too, started to bustle around with an entirely different expression on her face from the one she had had a little while ago. She was going to have fun at camp, so that she could help with that baby when she got back. Wouldn't mother be surprised when she saw what she could do!

Oh, there was so much excitement!

"Look! look!" called out Jane. "Look, there's the new gym and dining hall. I did not expect it to be as big as all that. Now we can have games when it rains and at night. And there is Lady waiting for us! Why won't the driver open the door and let us get out? And old Joe is there, too. Look at him! He's beaming from ear to ear! I bet he's glad camp has opened and we have come. Mother thought my locker was too heavy, but you just watch. Joe will throw it on the truck as if it were a feather pillow."

Finally the door of the bus did open and out they all piled almost on top of each other. Such hugging and kissing and crying you never saw in all your life; but the funny thing was that the girls who were crying were the happiest. Those who did not quite know whether they were going to like it or not were just as solemn as owls, but they certainly shed no tears.

An earlier bus had come in from another town.

"Hello there, Fatty! But we can't call you 'Fatty' any more. What have you done to yourself? You look six feet tall. 'Shorty' will have to be your name."

Before 'Shorty' had time to turn around, someone from the rear had put her hand over her eyes.

"Guess who!" She called excitedly.

"I can't guess," and she jerked her hands down. Then more hugging.

"Oh Jane, where are you going to be? In what cabin? Do you know your counselor? Let's try to get together again this year."

But the girls all knew that they could plan nothing. Everything that Lady said went. And they knew she was fair.

It was all so wonderful to be in camp again.

THE FIRST CAMPFIRE

"THERE GOES THE BUGLE," THE GIRLS SHOUTED. THEY all knew what that meant. They were starved, positively starving. And oh, everything tasted so good, even the much despised carrots; and somehow they drank all their glasses of milk. There was no urging. They took it for granted that it was the thing to do to eat what was set before them.

After lunch, the rest period. Would they have a rest period the first day of camp? Yes; for lunch was no sooner over than Lady rose and said,

"Each girl has already been assigned to her cabin and to her bunk. You have had a tiring trip. Many of you were up late last night packing. I shall expect quiet for one hour. No, you won't all sleep; but try to. If you can't, you may read or write letters; but no talking with your neighbor. I know you have hundreds of things to say, but there will be time for all of that. You may stay in your cabin when rest period is over, and unpack and get everything ready for inspection. Then we shall have games in the new gym at four; and campfire to-night. Remember, you old girls have each been assigned a 'sister' to look after. Think up all the nice things that you can do for her to make her feel at home. You know how you felt when *you* first came to camp. You may go now."

So with arms around each other, they walked out of the dining hall.

The afternoon came and went, with the expected ups and downs of the first day at camp. Some girls did not like the cabins they were assigned. Some did not like the girls they were put with. Others wanted the same counselor that they had had last year. While others were happy with anything and everything. And so the day passed, and evening came.

It was a perfect night, just ordered for the opening of camp. Even the moon was full; and the camp, with the shadows of the pine trees and the rippling of the lake, was like fairyland. The girls somehow caught the spirit of beauty, and were all in the mood, when the campfire was lighted and they sat on benches in a semicircle around it. Lady was dressed in white, with a dark blue scarf around her neck, looking her best. The girls gazed, and adored.

Fay stepped forward and said,

"Let's sing the camp song. You old campers all know it; and those who are here for the first time will be singing it before the fire dies out. . . . That's good; let's sing it again."

Lady's face beamed with pride as she looked over her girls who had been put under her care. They had such eager faces, and so trustful. Her heart was going pit-a-pat, more than any of the girls imagined. She was so anxious to say just the right thing, so that each girl would grow into womanhood in a wiser better way than if she had never come to camp. She had a great responsibility. She had heard so much about the way the teen-agers were behaving, that she was determined that no girl should leave camp without knowing the facts about life.

So she was going to start in at the very first campfire to let them know her plans.

Lady rose and started to speak; but the girls all burst into song. "She's a jolly good fellow." She lifted her hand and quieted them a little sooner than she usually did; and she looked a little more serious too. Some were beginning to wonder if they were going to have as much fun this year at camp. But it was not long before Lady was laughing, and telling all about the program of swimming, horseback riding and tennis, and what it meant to play the game fair and square. Still there was an undercurrent of something and she became a little more serious as she said:

§

As a rule, our first campfire is spent in singing and telling experiences of what we've done this past winter. But so many of you here are old-timers that I am going to start right in as if we had been here for a month. The summer is all too short for what we want to do this year. We are going to have just as much fun in every way, but added to that fun is going to be something very special. We are going to study the most interesting subject in all the world—ourselves. Each girl here is a book to study, and you are the ones to study the hardest to find out what is in those books. I am here to help you, the counselors are, too. Then we are going to have an expert, Dr. Marilyn Johnson, come and talk to us. She is a doctor who has worked with girls a lot. She is a mother and she knows how girls feel and think and what they would like to know about their bodies as well as their minds. We want to go home from camp knowing ourselves, so that each of us can better live with herself and know how to grow into the kind of woman she wants to be.

You want to be liked by the boys, and you want to learn about them, too, and how to act when you are with them. It isn't easy for the boys either. They don't know very much about themselves; they have to work hard to find out what makes them act as they do. And can't they act up,—so smarty, as if they owned the world and were created just to be admired! Did it ever occur to you that they sometimes act that way just to cover up how insecure they really feel?

They think they are 'no count'; and they even think that the girls don't like them! Isn't it funny that it should be like that! But it's true, for all of that. There is hardly a teen-ager, boy or girl, that does not have that inferiority feeling. But instead of acting inferior and humble, they just show off and make fools of themselves. If boys can't get attention because they play on the football team or excel in class, they try to get into the limelight by making a nuisance of themselves. Anything to be noticed.

And how else do boys act? Well, we'll have to admit that some are just as courteous as can be, stepping back for a girl to go into a room first, and even picking up a book that might fall. You would think that girls would do anything to get a date with boys like that, but the show-off type attracts so much attention that some girls just fall for it. *They* want to be noticed, too. You may hear older people say, "Oh, they are young. They'll grow out of it." Sometimes they do; and sometimes they don't. We all know men and women that no one wants to be with. They have never grown up. They are still show-offs.

I think some of you girls are old enough to think things through. You take hard subjects like algebra, English, history; and you have to use your brains to pass those courses.

So why not study this most thrilling of all subjects, yourselves, and how you grow physically, mentally and emotionally. Maybe we can find out what it is that keeps some folks from becoming mature men and women. When you grow up, you want to take your places in the world, fully equipped in every way.

How many of you have ever watched a little baby? [All hands went up.] What is it that the baby is most interested in? I mean a very tiny one. Mother? Yes, of course; but even before he cares much about his mother? Why does he cry? Yes, he is hungry. He doesn't much care who feeds him, just so he gets filled up with milk. And then he is so contented he just goes fast asleep.

A little later he plays with his toes, sucks his fists. He takes pleasure in his own body; but before very long there is somebody else that comes into the picture. You have already guessed it, his mother. Then his father, his brothers and sisters, and others that may come into the home.

Or, were this baby a girl, later on when she goes to school, she likes to play with girls her own age. She does not care much for the boys, I can assure you. They only tease.

But a little later, when she gets to be your age, she begins to be interested in being with boys. She likes to have them around. She likes to talk with one and then another. It would bore her if she thought she would have to go with one all of the time. She wants to look pretty, and she thinks about clothes a lot.

Then when she is a little older she wants to go with one boy, and only one. She does not enjoy being with the others. Then it is that young men and young women become engaged, marry and have children of their very own. Some are happily married; but we all know those who are not. Every single one that gets married wants to make a go of her marriage. So why doesn't she?

There are many answers of course. But there is one big reason for a great deal of unhappiness; and that is that either the man or the woman, has never really grown up. Perhaps neither has fully passed through all of the stages I have just told you about. To be sure, he doesn't remain a baby all of his life and play with his toes [a laugh from the girls]. But I dare say that every one of you girls knows a boy that loves himself more than anything else in the world. He is proud of his muscles. He will look at himself in the mirror every chance he gets. He wants everyone else, especially the girls, to look at him, too.

Now, every boy and girl should take great pride in the way he or she looks; but if this boy that we have been talking about, or any other boy or man, keeps on just loving himself and thinking only of himself, he is not going to love the girl he marries as he should. He is what we call a poor marriage risk. He has never grown up past that stage of self love.

I have taken a boy as an example. But you girls have heard how some temperamental movie stars are—thinking only of themselves, how they look, and how people go crazy over them. No, most of this type are not happily married, either. But you don't have to be a movie star to love only yourselves and keep that up till after you have married. Lots of ordinary folks fail just as badly.

Why do I tell you all about this? Some people might say that you are not old enough to understand; but I believe you are. Now is the time to study yourselves, at your very age, while you are growing up. If you know about life, it is so much easier to *keep from* making mistakes than it is to *undo* mistakes that you might make a little later because you did not know.

I realize that I have given you a lot to think about; but you will be so busy swimming and hiking and horseback riding that you won't have time to think too much. That is the best way to grow up after all, happy in work and play and having just loads of fun.

And now our evening song; and when taps comes, drop off to sleep and dream of tomorrow.

§

The girls had remained almost motionless for Lady's talk. Most of it was new to them, but they liked it. They liked to think of growing up, and knowing how to do it right. They all wanted to ask Lady questions, but they knew that would come later.

The stars were shining, the moon was high in the sky, and the shadows were still dancing, when the last of the girls dropped off to sleep.

WE WANT TO KNOW MORE

▣ ▣ ▣ ▣ ▣ ▣ ▣ ▣ ▣ ▣ ▣ ▣

LADY WAS BUSILY GOING OVER HER ACCOUNTS. SHE HAD gotten behind in her book work, and she simply had to shut herself up in her room and get that out of the way before the afternoon swimming meet. Feeling was running high as to which tribe would win; and she must be on hand in case any bitterness should break out. She did not enjoy those accounts. She much preferred to be with the girls. While she was adding up a column of figures, there was a knock at her door. She almost welcomed the interruption, but she did not expect what she saw. There stood a group of very serious looking campers with a look of anticipation on their faces which seemed to say, "You can answer all of our questions; and we really want to know." What faith the teen-ager has in us, if only we *did* know the answers!

"Well, girls, what can I do for you this time?" said Lady with a smile, as if time were no consideration to her at all.

Jane was the spokesman.

"We just wanted to talk to you. We want to know more about what you said to us last night at campfire. We don't understand some of the things that you told us."

Lady's office was well equipped for just such an intrusion. She had had girls knock at her door at other times; and they always came first, before any other business. Some sat on the big lounge, others on stools, while a few sat on chairs. They grouped themselves around her desk.

Lady began:

"I suppose I did try to tell you too much in one evening; but I just wanted to get the ball rolling, to make you girls think. We want to have plenty of time at the very beginning of camp to discuss all the angles of this important business of growing up. I am so glad that you have come to me so soon; and that you do have questions. We will try to answer them together; for I am sure some of you know the answers better than I. When I was your age, life was very different from what it is today; and so it is not always easy for me to put myself in your place. You will have to help me out, help me to see what your problems are. Well, who's first?"

Helen was the spokesman.

"I think I understand pretty well what you said about admiring ourselves and thinking that we are so wonderful—that clothes are the most important thing in the world, and the way we look. I know that is just about all I think about. I do want the boys to think I'm pretty."

"Now let me tell you something, Helen. I, too, hope the boys will think you are pretty. I hope you will always want to be well dressed, and never look like a sloppy Joe when you are at a formal reception; that is a most important thing in a girl's life. But when you're older and get married, if you still keep on thinking that your dress and the shade of lipstick are the biggest things in your life, that to have a baby might spoil your figure, then you have not grown up emotionally. We could all name some women who are just like that; and I'm afraid they don't make their husbands very happy. They have kept on loving themselves just a little too long. I wonder if you have my point. It's most important.

"Every one of these stages we pass through has its good traits that we want to keep. But when you have no other interests, and hold on to these too long, then it is that you cannot be the woman that you want to be, and that your husband will expect you to be."

"But, Lady, you spoke about the baby loving her mother. Surely you never outgrow that? But to tell you the truth, I almost hate my mother at times right now. I could kick myself every time I do; but still I do. She is so unreasonable, looks upon me as a little girl, and acts as if I had no brains in my head. And she tells me what *she* did when *she* was a little girl. What do I care what she did then? She lived in the age of the dodo. Anyhow, I'm not a little girl."

Some of the other girls looked almost shocked at this outburst; though if they had spoken truthfully, they all had felt the same way at times. Strange as it may seem, it did not bother Lady in the least. She smiled.

"I'm so glad that Helen has spoken out as she has; for she has saved me the trouble of saying the same thing, only in a very indefinite way. Each one of you girls, (if you are normal—and I am very sure that you are!) is going to rebel against your mother, at some time or other. But that does not mean that you are going to run away from home and be on your own, nor does it mean that you do not love her. It does mean that you have to begin to adjust, and be a very different kind of a girl in the same environment.

"You can't change your mother, much as you wish you

could at times. You can't throw your brothers and sisters out on the street. You have to live with the same furniture, which you think is too old-fashioned for words. How can you do it? Well, the answer is not easy. But you are on the right road when you begin now to think about all of this, and to learn to know yourself, what makes you act as you do, and why you have these strange thoughts.

"You don't have to be told (for you know it already) that you belong to that much-talked-of group, the teen-agers, that gives not only your mother a headache at times, but also your teacher, and anyone else that has anything to do with you. And, oh, how much they all want to help you! They make mistakes, of course. They say and do the wrong thing; but they are really interested in you, and want you to be happy.

"But let's get back to your mother, and what we were talking about last night. Even if you don't like your mother at times, you still love her. And I want you to believe me when I say it is nothing to worry about if you rebel a bit at the dress you are told to wear. You are not a little girl any more. You ought to be choosing your own clothes. You ought to be fixing up your room in a different way from when you were a child. Talk this over with your mother sometimes, when she is in a good mood and you are feeling good, too. It will amaze you the way she will swing in and help, instead of hindering. But when you get mad, and then she gets mad and flares back, what have you accomplished? Absolutely nothing.

"About this mother-love stage of development, there is more to that than meets the eye. If when you are eighteen or twenty you would rather be with your mother than go out with a boy, then you are lingering too long in that little girl mother-love stage. It is far more natural for you then to want to be with the boys than to want to go places with just your parents. Always, always you will love your mother, more so as the years go by. But if, when the time comes that you want to get married, you feel you must live with your mother or have her come live with you, or at least be near enough so she can tell you what to do, then watch out! There is a danger signal ahead for an unhappy marriage.

"The same thing is true of the boy. Even more so. Beware of the boy whose mother is his only real interest, or whose mother hovers over him and wants to be the one to whom he constantly turns. Better leave him alone; for he is a big marriage risk. We all admire the boy who is thoughtful of his mother; for it is absolutely true that he will be thoughtful of his wife. That is a very different thing from what we call a 'mother fixation.'"

"Oh," sighed Helen, "I feel better now. I thought I was the only one who got out of patience with her mother, for other mothers always seem to know what to do better than mine; but as I think things over, I would not want to exchange her. I'm going to write her tonight and tell her how much I love her, for I said so many mean things before I left for camp. I'm going to tell her how much better I'm going to be when I get back."

"Better keep that as a surprise," said Lady with a smile. "The battle is not won yet; but it will be."

The girls were reluctant to leave, but it was time for swimming; so Lady pushed them out of the door. "More another day."

When they were outside they saw the girls all running to the lake. There was great excitement over who would be the winner. Helen and Jane held back a bit as they walked along together.

"I don't know whether I ought to go in swimming today or not. This is my first day. Mother says I shouldn't take a bath even, at that time of the month. I feel perfectly well, though," said Jane.

"I know one thing. I wouldn't dare to go in swimming; for I have cramps if I do the slightest thing the first day. I just have to take a day off. Look at Edith. She pays no more attention to it than if it did not exist. I really do envy her. I wish that Dr. Johnson would hurry up and come to camp and talk to us. Then we could ask her all about this; for she would really know. I think camp is wonderful this year. I never dreamed we were going to have all these interesting talks about things I have wondered about for so long."

Lady was hard at work again over her books when the phone rang. It was Dr. Johnson. The girls heard her say (for the door was open), "Yes, indeed, tomorrow night will be fine, the sooner the better. We'll be looking for you." Lady was delighted that she could come so soon after the opening of camp. She was very anxious for the girls to have time to think things over. It takes time to grow. It takes time to learn how; and it takes time to have long thoughts, and dreams of the future, when wedding bells will ring.

DR. MARILYN JOHNSON SPEAKS

□ □ □ □ □ □ □ □ □ □ □ □

"YES, GIRLS, DR. JOHNSON IS COMING TONIGHT. SHE IS going to talk in the gym at seven. Just wear blue shorts as usual. It will be very informal. But I want every girl to be there. Pass the word around; and put a notice on the bulletin board."

Even the old girls did not know quite what it was all about. This was something new at camp, to study about themselves. They did not have to be urged to go to the gym. They were there, and ahead of time. They sat on the floor in groups, not in a formal circle as they sometimes did.

Lady and Dr. Johnson each had a chair; and Lady had placed a little stand beside Dr. Johnson's, thinking she might be using notes. But no indeed! She stood right up and started to speak, just as if she were talking to each girl, and to her alone. Everybody loved her at once.

She began by telling a lot of stories. The girls laughed heartily and almost began to think she had forgotten she was a doctor. But before long she became quite serious, and so did they. This is what she said:

§

I'm going to talk to you this evening exactly the way I

talk to my medical students. I'm going to tell you just what I tell them, the whole story of how your body works, at your age. I'm going to use scientific terms, too. If you understand what they mean (and I'll explain each one as we go along), it is so much more definite and satisfactory than using baby words or more familiar language.

In the science books you girls are spoken of as "adolescents." That means "becoming adult." You prefer to think of yourselves as "teen-agers." But whatever you call yourselves, you've probably noticed that certain changes are taking place inside you, though probably you haven't stopped to think too much about it. You don't understand what they are or what they mean, though you do feel them happening. See if you don't know what I mean.

You used to pay little or no attention to boys, except to think them nuisances when you had to play games with them, or to hate them when they got big enough to tease you when you wanted to play with the other little girls. But a change has come over you lately, in the way you look at boys, and think about them; not all of you, but most of you girls who are here listening to me tonight.

They're probably even more noisy, and bothersome, than they used to be. At least, older folks think they are. But to you they have become interesting; and you want them to find you interesting, too. You don't mind their being clumsy, and boisterous, and not too polite. You are beginning to think of them as romantic, maybe a little bit mysterious even, certainly desirable to have around, even though you are not always quite certain how to act so as to make them *want* to come around. You may even actually begin to dream about them, and not only when you're asleep, but sometimes when you are wide awake, too, apparently! (Here the girls laughed, rather nervously).

Then, too, you are beginning to think about what is going to happen to you when you get older. Of course, every one of you expects to get married, even those few who insist that they don't; and equally, of course, you expect to have children. You don't know just who your husband is going to be, that you'll decide on later; but somehow or other, whenever you dream about your hero he vaguely resembles some one of the boys you know, or have been hoping to meet. You don't know how or when all this is going to happen. You only know that it *is* going to, some time in the future.

Along with these changes in the way you *feel,* you and your girl friends are beginning to notice a change in the way you *look.* Up to now, you've simply been growing bigger, and taller, and heavier. But of late, you've begun to notice slight but quite definite changes in your figure. Some of you girls are fatter, some not so fat; but it's not only that. Your hips are a little broader; your legs are getting longer; your breasts, that used to be flat on your chests, are rounding out. In other words, you are beginning to have some curves, instead of being all angles, the way you were as long as you were little girls. You have noticed, too, a little growth of hair beginning under your armpits, and in your groins. What do you suppose it is that causes all these strange changes to happen, in your bodies and in your minds, too?

Well, there are two little glands in the body of every girl or woman, one on each side. They are called ovaries, because their job is to manufacture and turn out a tiny egg every month. The Latin word for egg is *ovum.* Nothing mysterious about that, is there?

But they also manufacture something whose action *is* mysterious, and hard to understand. It's called estrogen; and it has the magic power of turning a girl into a woman! It not only makes you *look* like a woman, instead of like a little girl; it makes you *feel* and *think* like one, too, and begin to dream about growing up, and falling in love, and marrying, and having children. And along with all these new ideas go a lot of vague, rosy-tinted dreams about boys, and later on about one special boy. This is what we call romance.

Later on we'll talk about these changes in your thoughts and feelings, and what they do to you, and how they can help you if you understand how to manage them, and how they can harm you if you don't. But tonight I want to stick to the physical side, and explain to you a little more about what happens in these two manufacturing plants, the ovaries.

I told you a moment ago that every four weeks or so one of them sends out an ovum. This is a tiny microscopic speck, about 1/125 of an inch long. Now where do you suppose it goes to?

Well, it is wafted right into a tube called the Fallopian tube (after Fallopius, a 16th-century physician) that takes it into the womb, or uterus, an organ about the size and shape of a pear, situated in the center of the body. Here it stays for a few days, and then is detached and thrown out of the body. Along with it goes some of the lining of the uterus which had become thickened in order to receive and take care of it, and a certain amount of blood.

When this happens, and it takes four days, more or less, for the discharge to be over and done with, we say that a girl is "having her monthly period." Some people still call it her "monthly sickness"; for it used to be considered a time when a girl was expected to be sick, and to avoid all sorts of exercise, or even activity of any sort.

But we are going to use the scientific term here as everywhere else, as I told you we should; so we'll say that she is menstruating. And as we're going to be accurate as well as scientific, we won't call it a "sickness," nor yet "the curse," as some girls foolishly term it.

The age at which they begin having their monthly periods (what folks call "the beginning of puberty"), is very different in different girls. Probably most girls start between the ages of 12 and 14; but they may begin as young as 10 or 11, or even earlier. And some girls don't commence to menstruate until they are 15 or 16 years old.

Some girls are, as we say, perfectly regular. They flow for four days, every 28 days, right from the start. Others, while they eventually become quite regular, may skip a month or two, at the beginning. The duration of the flow, too, varies from one day to several; and it may be very scanty, or quite profuse. These variations should not be looked upon as indicating that anything is wrong. Such wide variations are perfectly possible within the limits of the normal.

What is *not* all right, and is certainly not to be neglected, is this business of painful menstruation that troubles so many girls. To be sure, it is not at all unusual for a girl to have a moderate amount of discomfort, and even a little bit of pain, especially at the starting up of the flow each month. The uterus is sometimes tipped at an angle with the vagina, into which the flow is emptied; and that makes it a little difficult for the discharge to escape. But any pain or discomfort is sufficient to make it the business of any mother to take her daughter to her family physician. He can usually detect the little irregularity that is the cause of the discomfort, and correct it without much difficulty.

I imagine that most of you girls probably had some hazy idea of what menstruation was like, before it started. But many of you dreaded it, without any very definite knowledge as to what it was all about. Even if your mothers had told you all they knew about it, as more and more mothers are learning the advisability of doing, you may have dreaded it. Perhaps you feared that it might mean severe pain, or the loss of a dangerous amount of blood, or something else equally frightening—but, as I can now assure you, equally untrue!

On the other hand, a number of you, instead of dreading the starting of your monthly periods, have looked forward eagerly to this as a sign that you are growing up. And indeed it is—one of the first signs that you are leaving childhood and entering girlhood. You want, of course, to enjoy being what you are, as each day comes along; but life would be dull indeed if we could not anticipate the future with keen pleasure.

Girls sometimes worry if they "skip a period"; and think they ought to do something, like taking a hot bath, or taking some medicine, to "bring it on." There are several things that may cause such a failure of a period to come at the expected time. We'll talk about that at our next get-together

In the meantime you may wonder, as you have probably often wondered in the past, what all this rather bothersome business, that is sometimes embarrassing and often decidedly inconvenient, is designed for. You may be sure that it serves a useful purpose. Nature seldom or never does things without good and sufficient reason. But it's too late to go into that big subject tonight. Next time I meet with you, we'll take that up, and discuss some of the interesting things you'll want to know about it. But for now, goodnight.

THE MYSTERIES OF LIFE
ARE EXPLAINED

□ □ □ □ □ □ □ □ □ □ □ □

To HAVE DR. MARILYN JOHNSON TALK TO THE GIRLS SO frankly and clearly was an experiment at camp; and if the truth were told Lady was a little anxious as to how it would be received. But her fears were all unnecessary. The girls chatted about Dr. Johnson's talk with great interest, as they should have done; but not once did she hear a vulgar remark or a giggle as if knowledge were funny. They were eager to be told more. Lady thought it wise while their thoughts were on the lecture to have another talk follow immediately; and so it was arranged for Dr. Johnson to come the next night. There was no need of any introduction, so she began:

§

You will remember my telling you about the journey taken by the ovum that one or other of the ovaries produces every month or so. I told you that it travels along the Fallopian tube till it enters the uterus. It clings to the inner wall of the uterus for a few days, and then is washed out along with the rest of the menstrual discharge.

But sometimes the ovum is *not* discharged. No menstrual flow takes place; and the ovum continues to cling to the wall of the uterus. This is because something very special has happened to it, which makes it a very important bit of matter, indeed. But before I tell you what that something special is, I must explain to you something else, about which you have undoubtedly wondered. That is, just how boys differ from girls.

I don't mean in their looks, or their actions, or their clothes, or the part they play in life. I mean about the workings of their bodies, and how they compare with some of the things I told you last time about *your* bodies. One of the amazing things about us, men and women, is that, although we are so different in almost every way, there are a number of things about us that are astonishingly similar. You'll see what I mean by this confusing statement in just a minute; for I'm going to tell you in detail some of the similarities, and some of the differences.

For example: The girl has two almond-sized glands, the ovaries, that manufacture the female elements, the ova. The boy has two similar-sized glands, the testicles, that manufacture the male elements, the spermatozoa, or sperms. But the ovaries are situated *in*side the girl's body, while the testicles are carried in a pouch called the scrotum, *out*side the boy's.

Another difference is one for which it is hard to see any reason. The two ovaries, between them, produce but one ovum a month, whereas the testicles are producing hundreds of millions of sperms, and producing them constantly.

Again, the ovaries pour out a secretion, estrogen, that changes a girl into a woman. The testicles pour out a secretion, testosterone, that changes a boy into a man. Each of them, in addition to changing a child into an adolescent and then into an adult, makes one sex interested in being with the other, and in coming into close contact with the other; and each of them makes both the young man and the young woman want to have children. But there is a difference here too, as well as a similarity. For while the desire to have children and the thought of them (even though of course she does not want them at once) appears fairly early in the adolescent girl, it appears much later in the adult man. This difference has quite a different effect when the question of marrying comes into the picture.

Now ever since I mentioned that sometimes something very special happens to one of these ova, in the course of its journey from the ovary to the uterus, so that it doesn't have to be thrown out at a period, some of you girls have been wondering just what that something might be. Some of you older ones have guessed it already, I imagine. Now I'm going to tell you what it is.

When a man and a woman love each other enough to forsake all others and cleave (that is, cling) to each other as long as they both shall live, they marry. They have made love to each other, during their courtship and engagement. But after they have become man and wife, a further experience, which is called intercourse, awaits them.

If they desire it, their love-making may sometimes have a wonderful result. One of the millions of sperms I told you about joins the ovum that is traveling toward the uterus. When these two tiny life-bearing particles, a male sperm and a female ovum, unite, we say that the ovum has been fertilized. Another way of expressing it is to say that the wife has become pregnant.

The result is the very first stage in the life of a new human being, with all the possibilities of attainment that lie before a completely separate personality. In nine months, or there-abouts, this tiny mite will have grown large enough to exist separately from its mother. Then it will be expelled from the uterus, where it has been so carefully nourished and kept warm, right close up under its mother's heart.

So far I've been telling you a great truth. But to be abso-lutely fair and square with you, I'll have to confess that what I've told you is in reality only half the truth, the beautiful half of a truth that has a very unhappy, sordid, dreadful side. I've told you that this business of creating a new life is the result of the act of a man and a woman who love each other well enough to become man and wife for life. The ceremony that blesses their union is a beautiful piece of consecration; but it in itself does not have anything to do with creating the new life. It is intercourse alone that makes that possible.

Now the other half of this wonderful truth is, that it some-times happens that two people who do *not* love each other at all, or who love each other without having any right to have the experience we have been talking about that creates a new life, because they are not married, try to get it without any regard to whether it is right or wrong. What they are after is the physical sensation and thrill that they expect to get out of the experience; and the last thing they want or expect is to create a new life as a result of it.

In fact, they usually take what they have been told are precautions that will insure that this will *not* happen. And sometimes these precautions are successful. But sometimes it happens that they are not. And then, a terrible thing takes place.

The woman (often she is just a girl), becomes pregnant, and a baby, whom society brands as illegitimate, is born.

Then the unfortunate involuntary mother is flung out of her place in the world; and faces all sorts of grave problems.

Now since the plight of the unmarried mother is so tragic, and since the man is condemned so by his conscience and by society, people who commit this immoral act are usually very fearful lest pregnancy take place, in spite of the precautions they may have taken. And one of the earliest signs of pregnancy is skipping a period.

For this reason, girls who have always been regular sometimes become terrified if they happen to go over time. They have never been told, as every girl should be told, that this is not necessarily a sign of pregnancy. It may be due to fatigue, anemia, traveling, or any of several other things.

Girls who do not know what I have told you, that intercourse is the only way pregnancy can be started, sometimes become panic-stricken, especially if they have been indulging in heavy petting, with prolonged kissing. They will turn anywhere for something to stop the supposed pregnancy. To meet this situation, and make an evil profit from it, an almost unbelievable practice has grown up.

Unprincipled doctors, and equally unprincipled women, offer to give medicines, or even to perform a criminal operation, to bring on an overdue period and break up the supposed or actual pregnancy. Law and religion both consider this murder of the unborn child. And since it may kill the pregnant girl also, or make her an invalid for life, you can see how foolish it is for a girl who has skipped a period to do anything except go to her doctor, and follow his advice. He can put her fears at rest. But now to get back to what we were talking about before we got off on this unpleasant but important subject.

I hope sometime I may get a chance to tell you girls about how the tiny life grows steadily larger during the nine months until at last it becomes mature enough to live by itself, without the constant warmth and nourishment that have been in evidence during this whole time. Then one day, by some mysterious arrangement that no one has yet been able to explain, a signal comes to the bodies of the baby and his mother announcing that the time has come when they must separate. This act of separation is known as confinement, labor and delivery for the mother, and as birth for the baby.

You girls may have overheard older women talking, when they believed that you were not within earshot, about the terrible times some woman had to undergo when her baby was born. As a result of this loose talk, some of you may have come to look forward with dread to the experience, in your own case.

This is just too bad, because it is so unnecessary for you to have been scared this way. Advances in the practice of medicine, and new discoveries in the way of useful drugs, have robbed childbirth of its terrors. Even the "labor pains" you may have heard older women allude to, are now better and more accurately known simply as "contractions" by which the baby is carried along on his way to the outside world. Expectant mothers are now taught how they can help themselves; and many who have had one or more babies, even look forward with eager anticipation to going through the experience again.

It used to be considered out of the question for any girl to be told anything about how babies were born, or how their bodies were formed so as to perform this very necessary function. Boys and girls were given the impression by their elders that it was almost wicked for them even to think about how boys differ from girls. And never, never should a girl have the faintest idea of what takes place in marriage so that a new life can be created.

You girls of today are indeed fortunate. For lack of knowledge about the facts of life is no longer considered a sign of innocence. Instead, it is rightly known to be gross ignorance. Immorality is frowned upon today as it was in those days, when girls did not know what the term meant. Now that you do, it is up to you girls to set up standards so that marriage will never be debased from the sacred relationship God intended it to be.

You know now, if you did not know it before, that heavy petting and experimenting can so debase it. So upon you rests the responsibility of keeping motherhood in its rightful place, as the greatest experience a woman can have. It has been truly said that "the race moves forward on the feet of little children."

Right now, here in camp, you are preparing yourselves physically and spiritually so that when you are the mothers of tomorrow, the world will be a better place to live in because of you. As you keep yourselves fine, you influence every boy that is your friend. Yours is this trust. I believe you will keep it.

MARY ANN RUNS AWAY

THERE WAS A BANGING AT LADY'S DOOR, NOT A MERE knock. Before she could say, "come in," the door was pushed open and Kay, out of breath, gasped,

"Lady, is Mary Ann here?"

"No, why?"

"She went down to practice archery; and when her turn came, she was nowhere to be found. One of the girls discovered a note in her cabin signed 'John.' It said, 'Meet me under the oak tree at four and we'll go for a ride.' "

Lady jumped up, startled.

"Who is this John? Do you know him?"

"Yes, I am very sure he is the one that drives the laundry truck. One of the girls saw Mary Ann talking to him the first day of camp."

"Do you know what oak tree he meant?"

"Yes, it is that great big tree down by the lake, near those dense woods."

"Take your car and swing around there. Swing around everywhere at once! But say nothing to the girls yet."

"But, Lady, the girls already know everything. The news spread around camp like wildfire."

"No time to waste. Hurry!"

So Kay ran out of the room while Lady tried to compose herself, and think. She had anticipated trouble with Mary Ann from the very first; but she had hoped to win her, and certainly did not expect anything to take place quite so soon.

Supper time came and went, and no Mary Ann. The girls whispered in groups in subdued voices. The camp songs somehow did not go over very well. No one was in the spirit. An awful thing had taken place and the girls did not know what was going to happen, but if the truth were told they were having the time of their lives with all of this excitement.

What went on behind closed doors with Lady and the counselors no one knew. But they all went to bed and there was no Mary Ann. She had not gone home, for Lady had phoned her mother. But about eleven o'clock that night Mary Ann slipped into her cabin. She had thought she could get into her bunk unnoticed but Fay, her counselor, was still wide awake.

"Why, Mary Ann, I am so glad to see you," she whispered, lest she wake the girls. "Did you have a good time?"

"No."

"Well, Lady told me that when you came in she wanted you to go and sleep in her room tonight."

"I don't want to and I'm not going to."

"Oh, you know how sweet Lady is. She will be so happy to have you safely back. She was a bit worried, for you know how interested she is in you."

Fay took Mary Ann gently by the arm and led her out of the cabin, while all the other girls slept soundly. Lady was not asleep. She was sitting up by her phone, trying to read. When Mary Ann walked in, she just threw her arms around her and kissed her, and Mary Ann cried. Lady patted her and loved her a bit, made a cup of hot chocolate for her and gave her some of the cookies she always kept on hand for various and sundry occasions. She chatted about camp and what she liked best to do, but both knew that all of this was killing time. So Lady did not mince matters, but came right to the point.

"Now, dear, tell me all about it. What made you run off without permission? Where did you go? And what happened? Had you ever known John before you came to camp?"

"Well, I just got tired of being cooped up with all these girls. Some may think it's fun to go swimming and play tennis; but that's not what *I* call fun. I want excitement and romance and a good time."

"And did you have a good time?"

"To tell the truth, no. I wish I had never run off. I hope I shall never see John again as long as I live. I hate him!"

"Now tell me. Where did you go, and what did you do?"

"I met John under the oak tree, and he told me to hop in his car and we'd go for a ride, that he'd get me back in time for supper, and no one would ever know that I'd been away. It was a beautiful day for a drive; so why shouldn't I? We drove and drove all over, and then he took me for supper at the Piggie-Wiggie House. After supper he said that he thought it would be fun to dance a bit. It was a little rowdy, and I didn't like the looks of the girls there, nor the boys and men, either. I also thought of my mother, and camp, and what you all would be thinking if you could see me. But I had not danced in so long! It really was fun, in a way.

"About nine, I told John I thought it was about time to go back to camp, so that I could slip in and no one would see me. He said 'No, let's spend the night here. I'll get you back before anyone wakes up, and no one will know about a thing.' But I did not want to. I told him I *had* to get back; that you would be worried. I saw no sense in spending the night. He begged and begged me, but I ran out and jumped into the car. It was dark coming home, and I didn't enjoy it. He kept putting his arm around me and hugging me, and then he would give me a kiss. I had never had a man really hug me like that before. And all at once he drew the car up to the side of the road and stopped. I said, 'What's the matter? Is there a puncture?' He did not say a word, just hugged and kissed me more and—

"And what else?" said Lady, trying to act composed.

"And I began to get scared. I don't know exactly why, but I began to think about what Dr. Johnson had told us and I did not know what was going to happen next. I got so scared I jumped up and screamed at him, 'Take me back to camp! I want to go home!' This kind of brought him to his senses; and he sat back in his seat and stepped on the gas, and we started. I thought we would *never* get back to camp over that long road. He did not talk to me much, just acted hateful, and said that he was never going to take me out again."

Lady was still composed in her manner; but she was not satisfied with the whole story.

"Mary Ann, I want you to answer me one question very honestly. Did John try to take off any of your clothes?"

"Yes, he jerked at my dress. But I got mad and told him to stop."

"Are you absolutely sure?"

"Absolutely and positively! No, Lady, nothing more happened than I have told you. I have not kept one thing back. I am telling you the truth and nothing but the truth. I know I did wrong." Mary Ann started to cry again.

"Please don't tell my mother; and *please* don't send me away from camp. I'll never, never do anything like that again. You had better tell the girls what I did, so that they won't go riding with John."

"You need not worry. John will never enter camp again with his truck. But there are other Johns. Every girl must know what the consequences may be, if she gets into a car with a man she does not know. Girls cannot be protected every minute. They must know facts and protect themselves. It is late, almost one o'clock. Here, take a pair of my pajamas, and roll up on the cot. You can sleep in my room tonight. We'll talk about your plans tomorrow."

"But please tell me that I can stay on here. Please, *please!*"

"Now don't you worry about that now. You just drop off to sleep," and Lady leaned over and kissed her on the forehead.

"Oh, Lady, you don't know how glad I am to be here, and not in that awful Piggie-Wiggie. That is an awful place. It really is."

"Now don't think of that any more; but dream about how you are going to win the tennis match tomorrow."

Mary Ann tossed a bit; but soon was sleeping so soundly that nothing could have disturbed her. And so Lady crept into her bed; but somehow she could not sleep quite so soundly. She knew the girls would have to be told more than Dr. Johnson had told them. Mere physiological facts were not enough. Mary Ann's conduct had proved that. She used to think that if girls knew the facts of life, nothing else was necessary. But now she knew better. She really had known, (though she hated to face it), that two girls had had to leave high school because they were pregnant. And they certainly had taken the prescribed course in hygiene. She was determined to give her girls the whole truth from every possible angle, make them not only know, but think things through; and if possible, inspire them with an ideal plus their knowledge. She kept thinking to herself, knowledge is not enough.

Lady was up a little earlier, if anything, than usual the next morning. She let Mary Ann sleep on. At breakfast she announced,

"I am glad to say that Mary Ann is safely back, and that everything is going to be all right. She did not get in till late; so I thought it best to let her sleep and get slept out. And, girls, I would appreciate it if you do not ask her too many questions. You all know that she ran off with John and took a drive in his car; and I can assure you that nothing really serious happened. Enough happened for me to want to have a real heart-to-heart talk about petting or necking, and how girls your age should really act with a boy. Mary Ann did a very dangerous thing when she went off with a strange man in his car. She has learned her lesson; but I want you to learn yours without suffering what she suffered. She thought she was going to have such fun; but it was far from it. Let's sit around the open fire tonight, and talk, and ask questions, and learn to know ourselves just a little better. I'll see you at seven."

WHAT'S THE HARM? PETTING

NEVER HAD THE GIRLS SEEN LADY SO SERIOUS. THEY KNEW that Mary Ann had run away, but she had gotten back. So what of it? They had taken rides with boys themselves. There was no harm in that. To be sure, she ought not to have gone without getting permission; but that was not enough to have made Lady act as solemn as she had all day. The girls wanted to get it over with, if she had anything awful to tell them. They heard at supper what they had expected to hear, that there would be a talk in the gym that night.

When they had assembled there was no delay. She began:

"Girls, I need not tell you what happened yesterday, for you all know it already; and Mary Ann has given me permission to use her as the subject of our discussion. She is right here with us; and I am sure she will agree with what I am about to say. Dr. Johnson has gone into great detail about what changes are now going on in your bodies, and how you differ from boys. She told you that when a young man and a young woman marry, one of the things they look forward to is having a baby of their very own. She told you how that baby was created, by the union of the male sperm and the female egg.

"I am afraid that Dr. Johnson did not make it clear that sometimes that very beautiful experience can be a most horrible one. Can you imagine anything worse than finding out that you were going to be a mother, when you were not married and you had never wanted a baby at all? There is not a girl here who does not know that two girls had to leave school last year for that very reason. Everybody tried to hush it up but everybody knew it.

"What happened? I knew one of the girls quite well; and she told me her story. She had been running around with one of the boys in town, who did not have any too good a reputation. But he had a car; and she thought it didn't matter, just to have a little excitement and fun. One night they drove out to a roadside café for supper. They each took a little drink, not much. No, they did not get drunk. They danced, and got excited, as a drink will make you; and before she knew it she was in his arms out in the car. He was hugging her and kissing her, just as Mary Ann said happened to her.

"But Mary Ann had not had a drink. She came to her senses and stopped short, and demanded to be taken back to camp. But this poor girl hardly knew what was happening to her. The boy would not let her go; and she did not want him to, at the moment. But when all was over, she was most unhappy, and he drove her home.

"She tried not to think anything more about it, but one day she went to the doctor's because she had skipped two of her monthly periods, when she had always been regular before. The doctor had the heart-breaking task of having to tell her and her mother that a baby was on the way. No, there was absolutely nothing else to do but to go through with the ordeal. It is positively against the law to take a life that has been started. And then, even if the doctor had been willing to commit a crime, it would have been a most serious operation, and might have cost the life of the girl. She just had to go away, always with this blot upon her reputation, and with the baby branded as illegitimate."

"Well, *I* think the *man* was to blame," one girl called out; "and I think he should have been put in jail! It isn't fair!"

"No. It is not fair, not at all. But you must know, and have it burned into your consciousness, that the girl is always the one to suffer most when, unmarried, she becomes a mother. It is something that I simply hate to think about—that such a wonderful experience for those who are married, can be turned into such a nightmare for those who are not married. Fun! Was that girl having fun? You need not answer, for you know.

"But the happy thought is, that it never need happen. Everyone can wait till married, both boys and girls, men and women. There is one rule to remember: Avoid prolonged petting; for it can only lead to trouble."

"What do you mean, Lady?"

"I mean just this. Hugging and kissing (petting) can be carried on so long that neither the boy nor the girl seem to be able to stop. And this is where drinking is always harmful. It makes your emotions go fast. You loosen the brakes and you lose control."

"Do you mean that you should never let a boy put his arm around you?"

"No, not at all. It is all right to see you young people go hand in hand. If a boy really cares for a girl, a good night kiss after a date or a handshake that shows a little feeling can hardly be termed going too far. But there is a very thin line drawn between what is going too far and what is not. Better err on the side of being considered too reserved, than of being too cheap with your kisses. And you do not have to act like a 'touch-me-not,' either.

"Every worth-while boy will respect you for this. The girl is the one that sets the pace. If she does not care how much the boy fondles her, and if she doesn't care how far he goes, there is no telling to what limits he *will* go. Yes, I blame the girls many, many times for allowing liberties with the boys. This is a new age, I know; and the girls have a freedom they never had before. But it makes me boil when I see a girl abuse that freedom, and encourage a boy to do what she knows he has no business to do."

Lady sounded almost angry. The girls knew that this was a pretty serious subject; and not one of them missed the point. As young as they were, they knew what she was talking about. She had the girls with her, too. They knew she was right; and they determined right then and there that they were going to have a happy marriage and not do anything beforehand to spoil it. They were going to help the boys to go straight, too.

The girls were all bursting with questions.

"Lady, do you think it is all right, when you are engaged to be married, to let a boy kiss you a lot?"

"That is a little different story. That goes into what we call courtship and marriage. You will take courses in that later. But I will say in answer to your question (and every question deserves an answer), that when young men and women of college age or over are engaged to be married, it is quite all right for more affection to be shown, but never, never should that line be crossed that we have been talking about, even though they are soon to be married."

"Can you get a baby if you just let a man kiss you a very long time?"

"No, that is impossible. There is only one way that a baby can be started; and Dr. Johnson has told us all about that."

"Do you think the reason that my mother is all the time fussing about my hitch-hiking, and getting into a car with a man I don't know, is because she is afraid that something like this might happen?"

"Yes, Edith, I *know* that is the reason, the main reason. She wants to protect you. For again, I hate to say it, but more than once a hitch-hiker has had just such an experience. And what is more, sometimes the nicest looking man will ask to take you home from school in his car. If you do not know him, it is wise for you to thank him and tell him that you are taking the bus."

"I want to ask a question about drinking. Do you think that one cocktail will hurt anyone? My mother and father take *their* cocktails."

"Again, Jane, I am not a very good one to ask; for when I am at a cocktail party, I always ask for ginger ale. No one cares whether I drink or not. Again, as with smoking, there is a big difference of opinion and people whose opinion I highly prize do not have my convictions about it. But we all agree on one thing, without a dissenting vote. And that is, that for teen-agers, any form of alcoholic drink is very, very harmful. You must know that your bodies have not matured, and your emotions are still easily upset. Why add a stimulant to make it harder to control them? For the next few years you are going to have a hard enough time to hold back tempers, and control yourselves in a hundred ways. And so, if anyone offers you a drink of *any* kind, be on the safe side, and ask for a soda."

A hand went up. Lady nodded to Nell.

"I wish you would explain one more thing about petting. It *must* be lots of fun; or so many boys and girls would not do it."

"Ask Mary Ann if she thought it was fun, the night she ran off with John. She is shaking her head 'no.' Yes, there *is* a certain amount of physical pleasure in prolonged kissing and embracing, but there is not much pleasure when you stop short. Then you have a sort of contempt for yourself for having spent the evening that way.

"Do your thinking first. Plan something that is a really good time. There is much more fun if you go out in groups, and have your boy and girl pleasures together at picnics and at the gym. Now is the time for you to meet a lot of boys and learn how to talk to all kinds. When you are older and reach what they call 'the mating age,' then you will prefer to be with only one boy. You'll like to talk with him about all kinds of things. You'll like to go to places of interest with him. Yes, you'll want to be alone with him; and you should. But right now, you are not at that age. You will have loads more fun by going in groups."

"Lady, when one of the girls at High left school last year to have a baby, I heard one of the older girls say that she was stupid, that there was no need for her to have had that baby at all. She could have prevented it. Is that true?"

"Yes, there *are* things that can be done to prevent 'conception,' as it is called. But there is nothing that is 100% sure. And I would rather not go into that now, for all of it is absolutely unnecessary, if you girls keep yourselves pure, keep yourselves with high ideals. No, that is not being old-fashioned; it is the very latest style. Have as your motto IT'S

SMART TO GO STRAIGHT. And don't you think a happy marriage is reward enough? To have a fine upright man in love with you, who wants you for his wife and to be the mother of his children, is worth a hundred petting parties. Don't you think so? And that is just what you have to look forward to, if you keep true to the ideals we have talked about in camp. And the most wonderful thing about being your age is that you have not done things to regret; that you can face life with knowledge and confidence. You are all so sweet and lovely now; and that is the way you can stay.

"Some of you girls may feel that I keep saying the same thing over and over. Maybe I do in order to get it fully across. And so at the expense, perhaps, of saying it again, I want to put upon you more responsibility in your relationship with your boy friends. Maybe there should be an absolute equality between boys and girls, but there isn't and you girls must face it. Boys are physically more impulsive. It is YOU. It is YOU that encourages them in heavy petting. YOU are the one that can keep not only yourself moral and straight but the boy straight also. And never forget, it is YOU that suffers the most, not the boy, when your petting goes too far. Maybe you will escape pregnancy by some good fortune. But you have endangered yourself just as much as if you had jumped in front of a rushing train in hopes that you could get across and not get hit. So look both ways before crossing the track.

"If any of you girls want to come to me privately and ask any more questions you know I am always ready to help.

"Good night and happy dreams. And may your prince come riding by and take you off, one of these days."

THE GIRLS TRY TO UNDERSTAND THEIR MOTHERS

▣ ▣ ▣ ▣ ▣ ▣ ▣ ▣ ▣ ▣ ▣ ▣

THE DAYS WERE JUST FLYING. CAMP WAS ALMOST HALF over. Some of the girls would be leaving then, and a few new girls would be coming. It did not seem possible that time could have flown so fast. Lady began to realize (so eager had she been to have the girls understand themselves in regard to the growth of their bodies, and all the changes that were taking place within them, and to know about boys in the same way) that she was almost neglecting one of the most important adjustments that any teen-age girl has to make—her attitude toward her mother. That subject was fraught with more explosives than almost anything else. Somehow the girls got along pretty well with their fathers, at their age; but their mothers were a constant source of irritation. And so at supper, when the announcements were being made, Lady said,

"Tonight around the campfire we are going to have an open discussion. And what do you think the subject will be? Our mothers! They won't be anywhere around; so we can just pick them to pieces all we want to. Be thinking about all the things your mothers do, that you wish they would *not* do; and all the things you wish they *would* do, that they don't.

It won't be so very long before you will be going home; and there you will have many a problem to face. Can't you hear your mother say, 'Now, dear, *don't* put on that bright lipstick. You are too young. And besides, school is no place to be looking as if you were going to a party.' " The girls all laughed; for how true, all too true, were those words.

"We'll toast some marshmallows around the fire, too, and sing. Better put on your sweaters, for it is just a little cool."

The girls began to buzz at once with each other as to what they liked and didn't like in their mothers. It was just as well that their mothers did not hear them; for unless they had been most understanding, it would not have made them very happy. Most of them were trying so hard to be good mothers; and then to see how they were failing, in the eyes of their daughters, would have made them sad indeed. But had they realized that every mother was in the same fix with her own teen-age daughter, it might have been a comfort. It just seems to be Nature's way, in this growing up process. It is not easy for mother or daughter.

The campfire burned. The girls were all seated around it and Lady began,

"First, I have a big surprise for you. I have just had a telephone message that Bessie has a little baby sister!"

There were "Ahs" and "Ohs."

"Let's give our camp yell for her; for she will be coming to camp, one of these days. Her father said that the baby was a little beauty, and her mother was so happy to have another girl. It is going to be hard now to keep Bessie in camp. She is going to want to go home and take care of that baby of hers. She can do so much to help her mother. It will be such fun to work with her."

"Well, I can tell you one thing. *I* don't think it's fun to have to look after my two-year-old brother, when I want to go out and play," exclaimed Jane.

"All right," said Lady, "Jane has started the ball rolling. She starts out with the first point as to what we don't like in our mothers. She does not like to be called upon as a baby sitter. Who next? Let's go right around, one after another, with just a sentence or two. All right, Helen."

"I don't like the way my mother tells me to fix my hair."

"Nor I," shouted another.

"I want to choose my own clothes, and my mother won't let me."

"I wish she wouldn't tell me that I am cold when I'm not and make me put on a warm dress that I nearly burn up in."

"Why does my mother have to tell me to turn off the radio, and say that I shouldn't be listening to such stuff, just because she doesn't happen to like murder mysteries?"

"When I go to a party, she calls twelve o'clock late to come home. Other mothers aren't like that."

"Oh yes, they are, for mine is; and I don't like it, either."

"I don't like the way my mother tries to look young, when she really is old. I heard her tell someone she is thirty-seven! And I'd like to know if *that* isn't old."

"I wish my mother wouldn't come in and giggle, when some of my boy friends stop by after school."

The girls were still going strong; but Lady thought that enough was enough; so she said,

"I think perhaps we have established the fact that mothers sometimes know how to irritate their daughters. Let's see now what we *like* in our mothers. Surely that shouldn't be too hard."

To Lady's surprise, there was absolute silence. Then one of the girls rose and said,

"Lady, you know we all do love our mothers. We do think they are wonderful. But please don't make us tell you what we like about them. That is so much harder."

That was an eye opener to Lady. She had thought that they would burst out with their likes even more quickly than with their dislikes. She had thought she knew girls pretty well, but she had learned something that night.

"I just want to talk to you a little bit about your mothers. I have met most of them; and I am a mother, too, you know. You are right in thinking that they are wonderful; and you are right when you say that they irritate you, for they do. Maybe you think that it should not be that way; but try as hard as a mother can, and she really does try, she rubs you the wrong way more often than the right, at your age.

"There is nothing abnormal or strange about that. It is perfectly normal and natural. You are growing up. You don't want to be considered a little child any more. But that doesn't mean that it is all right for you to lose your temper and put on a scene, when your mother suggests that you wear a dress that you dislike.

"Dr. Johnson has explained to you how and why you have so many conflicting emotions. One minute you are happy, the next you are down in the dumps; and then you flare up at the least little thing. In another few minutes, you are at peace with the world.

"It is hard to be your age. It is hard to grow up. Still that is no reason to be uncontrolled. We all know men and women who are married, who act just like that, and what is the result? Broken homes, and everyone unhappy. Now, right now, is the time that you can learn to get along with the man you are going to marry, even though you do not know who he is! You can do it by learning how to get along with your mother and father.

"I cannot command you to control yourselves. That would accomplish nothing. What I *can* do is to give a few suggestions that may help. When you are not feeling peeved about things, go over in your mind what it is that causes most friction between you and your mother. Probably clothes, and the boys, bring more heartaches than anything else.

"Just remember, she longs for you to look pretty. She longs for you to have the clothes that you like. She wants you to be popular. She saves her money to get you a dress; and when she buys it she thinks you are going to love it. When you look at it and turn up your nose and refuse even to try it on, how do you think she feels? I grant that it may not be pretty. But can't you work out some way so that you can both be pleased? She is eager to help you. She really is; but she doesn't know how. Maybe you can think up a new plan for choosing your clothes.

"Try very hard to be patient with your mother, if she does not seem to understand. You have been her little girl for such a long time. And then all of a sudden she finds that she has a young lady, and not a little girl any more to deal with. She can hardly believe that you are beginning to be interested in the boys. Maybe her first impulse is to keep you from them. She may think you are too young to have dates, or to go to parties.

"While she is learning to understand this new daughter of hers, she will be trying to meet you half way. So if you don't get all that you want at first, wait a bit. She will come around of herself; and then you will have so much more fun, than if you have had to fight it out every time. She will be trying to get your point of view, as you try to get hers. Every time that you and your mother can discuss things, and work them out without hard feelings, just say to yourself, 'There now! I'm learning how to control myself; so that when I get married, and my husband does something I don't like, I can just talk things over with him. I will not have to throw a book at him, the way they do in the movies!' There are no hard and fast rules entitled, 'How to get along with your mother!' *You* are a book. Your mother is another. You both have to study and learn."

Nell raised her hand. She wanted to speak.

"I think my mother is unreasonable. I am dead in love with a boy at school, and she says she does not like him."

"Are you 'going steady' with him?"

"Oh, no. I have never had a date with him. But every time I see him or think of him, I know I am in love. He is on the football team. I could just sit and sit and dream of him, and do nothing else. He smiled at me once in the hall at school. Oh, Lady, he is marvelous!"

"Why doesn't your mother like him?"

"She just thinks I'm silly to talk about him so much."

"This is what I'd do, if I were you. I'd meet and talk with some of the other boys at school, and get your mind off of him a bit. Keep him as a sort of dream-man if you want to; but get a few real ones into the picture. Your mother doesn't really dislike him; for she doesn't know him, any more than you do!

"What she *does* object to (and I think wisely so), is for you to spend so much time just daydreaming. Talk to some other boys; and see if you don't think it is more fun to have a real boy friend than an imaginary one. Maybe one day you will meet this football hero of yours; and that will be all right too. But in the meanwhile, have a good time with others."

Another girl raised her hand.

"What's your question, Dot?"

"My mother does not want me to smoke, and yet *she* smokes all the time. Do you think she has a right to try to keep me from smoking?"

"You have opened up a pretty big subject, one I wish I had all the answers to. You know I do not smoke myself; so maybe I'm not the one to answer that question. Your mother is not telling you that you can *never* smoke. She does not want you to smoke *now,* while you are growing up.

"Whether it hurts her or not, is an open question, with authorities on both sides; but no authority will say that it is good for either a teen-age boy or girl to smoke. Probably some of you girls have taken a puff or two from a cigarette; but I am very sure that none of you have the habit, else you could not have stopped when you came to camp.

"Ask smokers who have tried to stop, and see how hard it is. I dare say that for one reason or another your mother has tried to give up smoking, herself; and maybe she did for a short time. But she was so uncomfortable while doing so, that she felt it was not worth the effort, and so started it up again. I am not saying smoking is right or wrong, for your mother. I *know* it is wrong for a girl your age.

"And it is something for you girls to think about, before you start the habit. If you don't smoke, you save a lot of money that you can spend on pretty clothes. Then when you marry, and your baby is on the way, you don't have to wonder if it is going to harm the baby then, and during the nursing period. It is so much easier not to begin, than it is to be told it is wise to give it up.

"As I said, I am not a smoker, and so do not know the pleasure that you'd think *must* come from it, or so many men and women would not smoke. It is something you girls will have to decide for yourselves. But one thing I am absolutely sure of; and that is, that it is wise for you to decide right now that you will not smoke until you are through high school."

More hands went up, but Lady looked at her watch and said, "We'll get together again for more questions another time. But right now, off to your cabins, every one of you!"

MOTHERS TRY TO UNDERSTAND
THEIR DAUGHTERS

□ □ □ □ □ □ □ □ □ □ □ □ □

CAMP WAS IN FULL SWING AND LADY FELT THAT SHE could slip off and speak in a nearby town where many of the girls lived. The meeting was held in the beautiful home of Mrs. Ellis. It was called to order. The gavel fell and the president rose and said, "This is the last meeting of the Woman's Club for the summer. I thought it would be most helpful if we had someone speak to us today on what we may expect from our teen-age daughters when they return from camp. And don't we all shudder at the very thought! So I have invited Mrs. Rogers who has had much experience with the teen-agers to talk to us. Many of our daughters are in camp with her this summer. She is affectionately known as 'Lady' by the girls. And so Mrs. Rogers, the time is yours and it goes without saying that you have an eager audience of mothers."

No wonder the girls were crazy about Lady. She was so pretty and beautifully dressed. She held herself well and her hair was fixed just right. She had on lipstick, but exactly the right amount. Her dark navy blue suit was set off by a corsage. The mothers in the audience all envied her the easy

time they felt she must have in managing her own two daughters. She certainly must know the answers to all their problems. So it came as a surprise when Lady began:

§

First, I want to tell you we are here to discuss a subject that
no one knows any too much about. This is, how to be a wise
mother to a teen-age girl. The best we can do is to fumble
along together, and see if we can not help each other with
this age-old problem. It always comes as something entirely
new, when we wake up one morning and find we no longer
have a little girl as a daughter, but, instead, that much-talked-
of-creature, a teen-ager. A feeling of helplessness comes
over us.

I wish all of our daughters were here unseen, so that they
could hear us talk and so better understand us and our problems with them; for then they might realize that we are not
ganging up against them, to keep them down and prevent
them from having a good time. We really want them to have
fun, wear pretty clothes, and go out. There is so much talk
about parents' understanding their children; but many is the
time I've wished that children could understand their parents.

Did you notice I said "children" when I was really thinking
of the teen-agers? "Children" is a term we had better put out
of our thoughts and vocabulary at once. Yes, one minute they
do act like children; and the next minute we can hardly stand
it if they want to look as if they were sixteen! Can you imagine what a turmoil of emotions must be going on within
them, when all of that is taking place?

I need not ask what effect all of this is having upon us,
their parents. We are so anxious to say and do the right thing,
yet find ourselves in hot water all of the time doing and say-

ing the wrong thing. We feel that the world of today is really against us; that never did parents face such problems. And we all feel that our particular daughter or daughters are the most unreasonable of all!

Why is it that a girl can go off to the teen-age club and have such a good time; and then come home, kick over a chair, and fling herself upon her bed and sob? We want to comfort her; but she won't tell us what is the matter. Something so mysterious is taking place within her, that neither she nor anyone else can explain why. But, you say, we can't let this go on uncontrolled. We *must* discipline her somehow.

Now comes the hardest pill for any mother to have to swallow. Your daughter has reached the age of rebellion. If you are wise, you will let someone else help you in your task. You will always remain her backlog of security. And mark my word, that is no small rôle, if only you are willing to play it.

As you know, I am director of a camp for girls. You'd think that would be an ideal place for my own daughters. I tried having them there one summer. But never again! The next year off they went to a camp in another state. Why on earth they could not have had that teen-age adoration for me that the other girls had, still irks me every time I think about it.

Now why should this be? It is really not at all unreasonable. Our girls are growing up out of girlhood into womanhood. We mothers represent a bondage they don't like. We say "no" all too often, even if justifiably. They are thinking strange new thoughts they don't want to confide in us. But they must talk them over with someone—it may be with their girl friends, it may be with some older woman.

One day they're walking in the clouds. Everything goes

well at school. They just love the dress we suggest; sometimes they may even give us a hug of approval. Next day there's an outburst:

"I hate this dress. It's so short, and the awfullest shade of brown I ever saw. Whenever I wear it I look as if I came from an orphanage. I just won't put it on!"

It's snatched off and trampled under her feet. And what does her mother say then? If she is wise, she will know that this is no time to discuss the clothes problem. She will go quietly out of the room while her stomach is fairly churning with emotion, half with anger and half with a feeling of utter inadequacy. But before leaving she will say, quietly,

"Bessie, pick out the dress that YOU want to wear today. Whatever it is, it will please me."

Yes, I know what you are all thinking. "*That* is no way to discipline a daughter. If you give her an inch, she will take a mile next time." Suppose she *does* take a mile; and looks like a scare crow as she goes to school? Don't think for one moment that she won't "get it" from her classmates. They will tell her quickly enough that she is a sight. What *you* may say, matters not, for she thinks *you* old-fashioned; but she is very anxious to be admired by her friends, though their taste is not yours.

Another thing for us mothers to realize is that our daughters think that we are old in years, as well as old in ideas. That is not easy for us to realize. No, we may not have a grey hair, and the size of our dress is fourteen. We may be as youthful in our manner as can be; but the fact remains that, to the teen-ager, we are old.

You can remember so clearly how you felt on *your* first date. It seems like yesterday. You can put yourself right into her life and feelings; you know (or at least you think you do!) exactly what she is going through. But to her, you live in an entirely different world.

To begin with, you are married, and that alone is a terrible barrier. You remember so well being *un*married, and how it felt. But she has no idea about the experiences of a married woman. And so we have to be very understanding and sympathetic with her if she seems unreasonable, and fails to get our point of view.

Yes, I know what you are all wishing—that I would tell you what to do about this boy business. There is so much freedom now, and the girls just seem wild. They chase the boys and telephone them, instead of waiting for *them* to ask for dates. We feel that they are just spoiling the boys, that they will soon begin to think that all they have to do is to sit back, and the girls will do the rest, buy tickets to the ball games, and everything else. How can we get things back to normal once more, when the girls will be refined and the boys chivalrous?

Well, we will just have to admit that times have changed, and with them, our boys and girls. But let's not get too discouraged at the way things are today. Maybe this freedom we talk about is a good thing. It has waked us mothers up; and we realize as never before that the time has come when our girls, yes, our little girls, must know many things about life that we who were protected did not need to know.

I have many of your girls in camp this summer, and I have had a very fine woman physician come and talk to them and tell them about "the facts of life," and answer every question honestly, as they ask it. Every girl that leaves camp, I hope, will have a full realization about petting and what it may lead to; and a clear knowledge of the workings of her body. She will also have been told how boys differ from girls, and why. They will at least know a little better why they feel and act as they do. More than this, I hope to instill in them an ideal of womanhood; for knowledge alone is not enough.

§

Just then the telephone rang.

"It is for you, Mrs. Black."

The women instinctively stopped. They could not help but listen, and hear:

"No, I don't think you had better go. . . . How do you know he is a good driver? . . . Dear, that is a *very* old car. . . . What! *eight* of you pile in? . . . Well, be sure to get back before dark. You know your father. . . ." The conversation came to an abrupt end; and Mrs. Black returned to her seat with a worried expression on her face.

"Oh dear, what should I have done? Bill has just bought an old car." She did not have to say more; for every mother in the room knew what it was all about.

Some of the fathers had come down hard on their daughters and said "You cannot." But that hadn't worked. It had only made matters worse. It produced more problems, instead of solving the first. There was an almost audible groan in the room, as they faced life with all their teen-agers. And at the same time the teen-agers were probably groaning over their unreasonable mothers!

But Lady somehow gave them hope.

"It really isn't quite as bad as all that," she smiled. "We'll all live through it somehow. There is getting to be a partnership between mothers and daughters, as there never has been before. Mothers and daughters are trying to understand each other, and although there are still many clashes, now they are in the open and not behind our backs.

"No, this business of being a mother to a teen-age girl isn't easy; nor is it easy for the teen-age girl, either. Would you like to be one to-day? Not a single one of you would change places with her. Try hard to see the good things that she does; and even though you feel at times as if you could wring her neck, keep on praising her. One of these days you are going to hear her say,

" 'I have the most wonderful mother in all the world!'

"It may not come today, nor tomorrow; but it *will* come. Then you will feel a lump in your throat as you look at her in all her loveliness; and you will know that the effort was all worthwhile. Keep faith with her, that girl of yours. She is worth understanding."

The hostess rose. The meeting stood adjourned.

WHAT AM I GOING TO BE
WHEN I GROW UP?

□ □ □ □ □ □ □ □ □ □ □ □

IT WAS RAINING OUTSIDE; SO THE GIRLS ALL WENT TO THE gym for their evening talk. Lady was there waiting for them. As soon as they were seated, she began:

§

Many times this summer I have heard you girls discussing your future plans, and asking one another,

"What are you going to be, when you grow up?"

These have been some of your answers:

"Oh, I'm going in for nurses' training."

"I'm going to be a teacher."

"No, I'm going to take a secretarial course."

Perhaps one or two of you have said you wanted to be a doctor, like Dr. Marilyn Johnson. Some one of you will be sure to say,

"Oh, *I'm* going to get married," the tone of your voice rather implying,

"I don't have to think about earning my own living, or taking any special course, with a husband to support me. If I know how to cook a little, that's all that will be necessary." We'll consider all this in a little more detail.

Once that may have been sound reasoning. But it very definitely is not true today. Frankly, I seriously doubt if that day ever returns. Not all of you will come out and say that you are going to get married, that that is your one ambition in life. In fact, some of you will state very definitely right now that you are *not* going to marry.

But no matter what any of you plan in the way of a career, or a profession, or not being married, way down deep within you there is the desire for a home of your own; and you hope that some day your dream prince will come and take you to it. That is the way life is; you cannot escape it.

However, you must not think that if you remain unmarried, as some of you undoubtedly will, you have failed. We can all point to women who have never married, yet have done more toward helping others to succeed in life, than many a married woman who has not thought of helping others. Just being married in no way spells success or happiness.

Too many have leaped before they looked, and then regretted it all the rest of their lives. Nor is divorce any way out, as so many boys and girls think it is. It may be justified, in certain cases; but it is a sign that someone has failed, somewhere along the line. And none of us wants to be a failure.

But let's go back to our problem: What do you want to be in life? Right now, this summer, you are preparing for your career, in the best possible way. For don't think for a minute that after you get your high school diploma, you've been handed a ticket for successful living. Instead, it's a milestone; better still, it's a springboard for bigger and better things. For unless your life has been well spent, and filled to the brim and overflowing with every possible activity, in school and out, you will find yourself at a loss to know what to do when the day comes that we call Commencement.

Believe it or not, that is why you are at camp—to learn how to live when you get out in the world. If you learn to play the game fair and square here, you will play it that way when you are at college, or taking special training; and then, best of all, when you get married.

We all want to be liked, to be popular. But no one achieves popularity by simply wanting it, or by merely thinking about it. It is the girl who is so busy doing things, and thinking of others, that she has no time to wonder whether she is popular or not, who finds herself surrounded by the boys, and sought out by others who just like to be with her. She doesn't have to phone the boys for dates, or sit by the phone whimpering and whining and not knowing what to do with herself.

The girl who is going to succeed as a nurse, a teacher, a secretary or a wife, is the one that can excel in tennis, swimming and basketball, as well as in her school work. Above all, she is the girl who can get along with her friends and her family.

I know perfectly well that girls of your age are very conscious of your looks. You all want to be pretty. That is all right; you should. But remember, it is not always the pretty face that is really beautiful. I had a friend, when I was a girl, who was very homely. No one could deny that. She knew it; and she evidently determined that, because she was so homely, she would have to make up for it in other ways.

She did not take the attitude that she was a "nobody's darling," and sit back unloved. Instead, she realized that unless she offered something more to people, her looks would be a bar to her happiness. She worked hard at her studies, but she didn't stop there. She went into every school activity as well.

Above all, she went out of her way to do something for everybody with whom she came in contact, whether that somebody was the janitor, a teacher, one of the girls, or a little child she happened to meet on the street.

She was fortunate in having a keen sense of humor. She made a real effort to see to it that everyone had a good time at a party where she was a guest. Did she have dates? You may be sure she did. Today she is happily married, with a lovely family and home of her own.

Let's pretend that one of you girls always feels inferior to other girls. You are convinced you can't possibly amount to anything when you grow up. You are constantly comparing yourself with girls who get better grades at school. At camp you see those who can excel in tennis, or swim a little faster than you can. When you go to a party, you think that boys gather around them, and you are left a wallflower. You suffer more than most people think; for youth is not the happiest time of life. Perhaps an adult may say, "Oh, that is your age. You'll get over it."

But it isn't much fun feeling all these feelings, and thinking all these thoughts. You want to be like other girls, attractive, popular and successful.

Let me tell you a secret. Those other girls that you are envying are feeling and thinking very much as you are. They don't know what they are going to be or do when they grow up, either. They may be able to swim and play tennis better than you, but instead of being happy over that they feel they can't stand it because they are so poor in craft work or tap dancing, and you are so good at it. Maybe you didn't think of that.

And now what about you at a party? You think the other

girls are having the time of their lives, because you see them in the midst of a group of boys. Perhaps one of those girls looks over at you and sees you talking to just one boy. And what does *she* think? "Oh dear, I wish I were Alice [we'll call you Alice]. She is talking to the only boy here that I want to be with. I just know he is going to like her better than he does me." Is she happy at the party? Utterly miserable. She thought *you* were having a good time, and you thought *she* was.

I'll have to admit there are some girls who always have a group of boys buzzing around them. They have "personality plus," or "umph," or "it," or whatever you may choose to call it. But I am not going to admit that they are the most fortunate, or the happiest and most to be envied. Girls are often misled by this teen-age popularity, and so do not put forth the effort which it is going to take to be the really worth-while woman every girl wants to be. It is hard for you to realize that one day you will be grown up and actually called a woman. That is a dreamy, hazy future state, and perhaps none too attractive at the moment. You don't care ever to be like the average woman you know; but there are a few that you admire and want to be like. Think of them.

Let's look at a few of the things you do here that will give you the full life that you all want, a life of interest in many lines, and one that can help you to adjust to new interests later on. It is the eager mind that counts, the mind that keeps on learning always. Wouldn't it be a terrible thing if when you left camp you were to take away only what you had been taught here, and never cared to go out after new knowledge?

You play tennis here and swim, though you may never need those activities later on. The big purpose of all our physical activities is to train your bodies to be healthy, well formed and capable of carrying on the work that you will be doing some day. No matter what it is, you will need to be strong and attractive physically. You certainly want your keen mind to be housed in a beautiful body. Not one single day can be neglected; for every day you lay one brick in the foundation of the house you are to live in, called yourself.

Now suppose you make some big mistake. Maybe you've told a lie, or maybe you've said some very mean unkind thing. Maybe you have let a boy go a little farther than you wish you had. It may not have been anything really wrong; but anyhow it preys on your mind. What are you going to do about it?

First of all, let's realize that we all make mistakes. None of us go through life without doing something that we wish we had not done. That is part of this world of ours. But one mistake need not lead to another. We can learn by our mistakes, and sometimes climb up higher in helping others not to make the same ones. There is one thing that never, never helps. That is to brood, to keep thinking and thinking and feeling that you did wrong. Perhaps what you did wasn't so serious, after all. If you ever have that guilty feeling which is such a handicap to success, talk it over with some older person. If not your mother, then your doctor, your pastor or your teacher. The mere telling of it may make the whole thing disappear; and you will say to yourself, "How silly I was to worry over that!" It will make you feel so good to get it out of your system. Keep reminding yourself, that what you suffer and feel is not "just you," but that everyone is feeling like that, in one way or another.

So far this evening we have talked about what you want to *be* when you grow up, the kind of girl that can make a success in life. There is not one of you here that does not have something in mind that you want to *do,* but you change from one thing to another; and that is the way it should be, right now. One day you may think you want to be an artist, the next day you are sure you want to be a movie star or a model in New York. Even the Army or Navy may appeal; or one of the good old stand-bys, teaching or nursing.

Never have girls had such wonderful opportunities. Now they may enter practically any field open to men. It has been proved beyond doubt that we are not inferior creatures; that we can compete successfully with men in just about everything. Now whether you want to enter some of these masculine fields, is a different matter. Right here comes a most important decision that you will have to make later on. Choose the training that *you* want, not what anybody else wants for you.

The other day I saw a cartoon that was very suggestive of the changing world of today. A teen-age girl said to her mother, "I think he is getting serious. Last night he told me he thought it was time that I was getting a job!"

Now what did that cartoon teach? Just this. The day has passed when a pretty face is enough to attract a man when he is looking for a wife. It may still fool some people; but they often live to regret it. Being trained so as to be self supporting is an insurance policy that should be a requisite for every wife, whether she ever uses it or not. After all, homemaking as a profession is a full-time job, surpassed by none in its importance; but it is inspiring indeed to see young couples today sharing in work so that they can make both ends meet, and in that way establish a home. And it is just as inspiring to see the young husband share in the house work, and in caring for the baby. Together they move forward.

There is a wonderful thing about growing up and planning your life at your age. What you do day by day is what counts. Each day is so very important. Right now in camp, and when you go back to school, you are becoming the girl of your dreams, and, yes, the girl that some boy will dream of, too, and one day will claim as his own.

Girls, you have been very good tonight to listen so attentively. For what I have been saying is not easy to understand; and it's very hard to put into practice. But I believe that my girls can do it; and, what is more, will do it.

Our camp season is flying, so make the most of it. Good night.

FRIENDSHIPS

A FEW EVENINGS LATER THE GIRLS, GATHERED FOR THE customary discussion, listened with even more than their usual attention as Lady began speaking.

§

Let's talk a little bit more about the boys tonight. Not that we haven't mentioned them before! But this time we want to think about the kind of a boy each one of you would like to have as a friend, if you could make him to order. Some of you have boy friends now, others will have them next year. There are a great many boys in high school, and a great many different kinds; so you'll have a wide variety to pick from. Maybe you think *they* should be the ones to pick *you*! Yes, they will. But you'll have a choice, too, as to which ones you want to be with.

I know it is quite the fashion these days for boys and girls to pair off. You want to feel that you really own the boy you are going with, at least for the time being; and you quite resent the idea of another girl's cutting in, and perhaps cutting you out! This is often a time of heartache for a girl, even at your age. But if you will look at things sensibly now and plan for them in advance, maybe you can avoid having some of those hard feelings, and enjoy being with boys, or *a boy*, next year.

You all know, of course, that you are definitely *not* at the age to get married. Then at what age are you? You are at the perfect age for meeting, meeting, meeting boys, so that you can really know them, and know their good traits, yes, and their bad ones, too. You want to study yourselves, and learn what it is that makes you prefer one boy to another, and why one boy is liked by the girls but isn't popular with the boys. Yes, one of the most important studies you'll take in high school is BOYS.

Your teachers may not agree with me in this. For you know you do drive them crazy at times because they feel that you are thinking too much about the boys. That may well be true in the case of many a girl; for there is nothing gained by just mooning around and daydreaming. That isn't studying boys. That's making a fool of yourself, and depriving yourself of the opportunity of getting ahead with your education, or of planning for some good times at a club meeting or game.

I've already talked to you about the good times boys and girls can have together, in a school play, a club, games, and other activities. The more you can be together in groups, the more fun and good times you'll have, and the more boys you'll learn to know.

But at every party there are always some who are going to want to slip off and go to a car and pet. You'll see more of that next year than you did last, for you'll be a year older. Many of the girls who'll be slipping off with the boys have not been told what you've heard from Dr. Marilyn Johnson this summer, and so do not know the risk they are running.

What they thought was going to be a little fun, may prove to be far from fun for some of them, when they have had time to think things over the next day.

I hate to say it, but it's not always the *boy* who is the one that suggests going out to the car. All too often it is the girl. But I have great faith in you girls. I really believe you have learned your lesson about petting, and what it may lead to. I feel confident that you are prepared now to meet any situation in which you may find yourselves, and act in such a way that you can be proud of yourselves. You'll find that the boys will respect you in a way you have no idea of. Is that old-fashioned, for a boy to respect a girl for doing what is right? *No*, a thousand times no! You are still the ones to lead, and set the pace, when it comes to setting up ideals and living up to them.

I read an article the other day lamenting what seems to me a very serious state of affairs, if it is true. It said that girls had become so lax, and were so free in their conduct, that the time had come for the boys to call a halt to this sort of thing, and set an example for the girls! If that can be said, we have come to a sad time indeed.

It will not be true, however, if a group of girls like you determine to hold to your motto, *"It's smart to go straight!"* Even one girl alone can exert a tremendous influence; and I don't mean one little pious prig of a girl, either. I mean the May Queen type. And if one girl alone can change things so at school, just think of what a group of such girls as you can do!

Speaking of May Queens, there was a study made of the social lives of the girls who had been chosen as May Queen in one of our large state universities. They looked into the social and personal life of each girl chosen by the student body for this important position, for each of the five preceding years, to see what type of girls they represented. There was not one girl that was known as a heavy petter! As you know, they were picked out from among hundreds of students, and had to be voted upon by the boys as well as by the girls. That certainly proved something that it is well for every girl to think over seriously. No, petting is *not* one of the requirements for popularity or friendship, but quite the reverse. And again I say that you need not act like a touch-me-not, either.

Well, if petting is not one of the requirements for popularity, or friendship with a boy, what is? I believe I would put common interests first on my list. But listen to me—this is a secret for you to hear, but not to tell. Suppose there is a boy you like a lot, but you can't stand his hobby, stamp collecting. He is simply wrapped up in it. You can fool him!

Get busy and learn a little about stamps. Maybe a friend who has a correspondent in some foreign country will occasionally let you have one from a letter just received. Another acquaintance who finds out that you are interested may give you a rare one. Before you know it, you are as excited over stamps as your boy friend is; and you are having the best time together after school going over his album with him. And the more stamps you get for him, why there you are with a good friend. And he never knew that you didn't like stamps!

Perhaps you know a boy who seems to want to go fishing all his spare time, while you wouldn't go for anything. Still, there is something mighty nice about him, and you like to be with him; and you hope that maybe he won't want to go fishing *all* his life. You may have something there; but don't sit down and wait for that day to come.

Send for a catalog of fishing tackle and sporting equipment. Find out about what fish have been taken from his favorite lake or stream. Get an interesting yarn about some old fisherman, or fishing village, and bring it into the conversation. Maybe this boy is rather shy, and a little bit afraid of girls. But when he sees that you are interested in the same things he is, he will open up and talk. You may be amazed at the good books he has read, that you can talk about. And presto, you have him as a friend!

No, there is no need for any girl not to have a boy friend. She may not have boys buzzing around her as some girls do. But after all, when the great day comes and the wedding bells are ringing, it is only one man that counts, after all. But of course the first boy friend you have is not usually the one for that occasion. You want to meet and know a lot of boys, to make sure that you are making no mistake. So you study boys and see how many you can attract as friends, now that you're in high school, by just finding out their interests, and getting interested yourself, and helping them with their hobbies.

It is quite an art in itself, this business of getting a boy friend, and holding him after you get him. There is nothing else quite as fascinating, at your age. But if you find that it is absorbing too much of your time or thoughts, keeping you from your studies or from joining in school activities with a real zest, then shoot up a little red flag in your brain as a danger signal, and get back to other things.

For a strange thing about all this, is that when girls show they are too anxious to attract the boys, they lose a lot of their appeal. A boy is far more likely to choose the girl who is not "boy crazy," than he is to want the girl who is.

One other word of advice. Think twice before you let yourself become the "aggressive girl." Boys don't like to be run after, as a rule, even though some of them may act as if they didn't mind. They still like to be the ones to ask for dates. That doesn't mean that you have to sit back and let the other girls get ahead of you, while you take the attitude that you don't care. You do care; and you should. And I can almost promise you that if you always look your prettiest, show your interest in some boy and his hobby, yet stay in with your group, you'll have a boy friend; and he'll be followed by another, and maybe by still another, as it should be at your age. If I were talking to a group of college-age girls who are seriously considering marriage, I might give entirely different advice. But to you teen-agers, it's a case of "the more, the merrier" when it comes to having boy friends.

But they are not the only friends you'll make. The girl who just runs around with boys and says she doesn't like girls is far from being the attractive person she wishes she were. She is not liked particularly by either boys or girls. Friendships formed now between you girls may go with you right through life. Of course a girl who is congenial with you now may not be congenial in a few years; and the same is true with your boy friends. But the possibility of making lifelong friends is one of the big reasons for coming to camp.

I don't mean crushes, where two girls "love each other to death," or where a camper "simply adores" her counselor. These are all right at your age. But sometimes you see two girls who, as they grow older, want to be with each other exclusively. They don't want each other to have friends among either boys or other girls.

If you suspect yourself of developing such an interest in another girl, no matter how fine both of you may be, then watch out! You might be entering into what the psychologists call "an unwholesome friendship." It doesn't take any great knowledge of human nature to see that such a friendship is far from desirable. For every girl should want the companionship of boys, and, too, want the companionship of one special boy as she gets to the age when she naturally should be thinking of marriage.

After a girl has had too close and exclusive a friendship with another girl, she may find it very hard to grow into the capacity for friendship and love with the other sex.

So keep your friendships with boys and with girls on a high level of companionship, working together, and playing together, and learning how to get along with each other. You may not realize it, in fact you may never have thought of such a thing; but it is true that in that way you will be laying the strongest possible foundation for a happy home of your own, when the right time comes along, in the not-so-very-distant future.

WHAT DOES GRANDMA THINK?

□ □ □ □ □ □ □ □ □ □ □ □ □

"GRANDMA, DID YOU HAVE FUN WHEN YOU WERE MY AGE?" asked Helen. She had run over to the dining hall where her grandmother was dietitian, and had stopped for a chat. Evidently Lady's talk the night before had made a deep impression upon her.

"Well, let me see," replied Grandma. "Of course I did have fun. But somehow, as I think back, I can remember more times when I was miserable than when I was happy. To begin with, my mother and I never *could* see eye to eye about my clothes. In those days, when a girl was twelve the length of her skirt began to get longer and longer with each new dress until she was sixteen, when it reached to her ankles."

"Oh, Grams! What a sight you must have been!"

"Yes. But each inch added meant that you were that much more grown up. We didn't buy our dresses in those days but had a dressmaker come to the house and make them. I can remember *begging* my mother to make my dress just a little bit longer than she thought best. She gave in to me, and it came almost to the middle of my leg.

"When I wore it to school, the girls all hooted at me and wanted to know who I thought I was trying to look like, the teacher or somebody. I couldn't get home fast enough after school. I threw myself across the bed and cried and cried."

"Why, Grandma, that was the craziest thing I ever heard of to be worried over. I would never have let that bother me."

"Well, my dear, maybe you wouldn't. But didn't I hear your mother and you discussing your evening dress? Your mother wanted straps over the shoulders, and you said in no uncertain terms that the girls would laugh at you if you wore that kind of a baby-looking dress."

"But, oh, Grams, you *know* that is different." And Helen jumped up out of her chair. Her face was flushed, and she looked as if she were just ready for a fight. "You *know* that is different. The way I look in an evening dress is very important. I want the boys to like me, and they won't if I look like a little girl, the way Mother wants me to look."

"You see," her grandmother said quietly, "you and I were not so very different when we were fourteen, after all. We were both trying our best to look grown up, and our mothers were trying their best to hold us back. I guess that's the way life is supposed to be, and then we strike a happy medium when we grow up."

"But Mother never had anything to worry about when she was my age. Daddy says she was always beautiful and always knew exactly what to say and do. She never did anything wrong when she went to a party."

"Now, listen to me," answered Grandma. "That may be what your father remembers. But *I* can remember something very different. I shall never forget the time I bought your mother the prettiest pink dress with little rosebuds all over it. She looked darling in it. But did she like it? No! She said she wouldn't be seen with such a dress on. She wanted a plain satin.

"We didn't have much money in those days, and I had bought the rosebud dress at a big sacrifice. But I couldn't bear to see her so unhappy, so I took it back and got the pink satin. And what do you think? One of the girls at the party had on that very rosebud dress, and everyone said she was beautiful, while your mother felt like the ugly duckling! She didn't have one bit of a good time."

"Why, Grandma," exclaimed Helen in amazement, "I never *dreamed* that Mother ever gave you any trouble!"

"It all just goes to show that your age is a hard age to live through, no matter what, whether a hundred years ago or a hundred years from now. Every boy and every girl seems to have to live through what is known as 'growing pains.' Some suffer more than others, but all suffer."

"I never thought of that before," said Helen, slowly and thoughtfully. "Isn't there some way in which a person can be happy *all* the time?"

"No. In this old world of ours that is a state no one is in, all the time. Life has its ups and downs. Perhaps people your age can go down deeper and then rise higher than at a later age. But we all have to learn to get along while we are unhappy as well as when we are happy. My mother used to tell me that years ago, and you will be telling it to your children years from now. You think that over, and we'll talk more about it sometime."

"But do tell me right now, Grandma, whatever happened when you were crying on your bed because your skirt was too long?" inquired Helen, as her grandmother paused.

"Well, my mother let me cry for a little while, and then

she said, 'Let's look at your dress. I can shorten it an inch or two right now, and it will look much better, I'm sure.' She didn't even say, 'I told you so.' She just made me feel good all over. And when I went to school the next day the girls all thought it looked perfect."

A week or so passed, and Helen came by to talk with her grandmother again. This time she was just on the verge of tears.

"Oh, Grandma," she burst out. "I had an awful time at the party last night. One of the boys was sitting beside me. I had my hand in my lap, and we sat there talking. He slipped his hand over mine and gave it a little squeeze.

"I snatched it away with a jerk, and he said, 'All right, if that's the way you feel, I'll go.' Then he jumped up and left me. I like him *so* much. He is one of the nicest boys I've met in a long time. I don't know why I acted like that. Oh, dear, oh, dear, he'll *never* speak to me again, I know. What *shall* I do?" and Helen started to cry as if her heart would break.

Her grandmother remained quiet for a minute or two. Then she said, "Let me tell you what happened to me one time when I was a year or two older than you are now, for in Grandma's day we didn't go out with the boys the way you do now. I was sixteen before I ever 'went with' a boy—we didn't say 'date' in those days.

"This boy walked home with me from church in broad daylight. Was I thrilled! My heart beat fast when he asked me if I would play tennis with him. He called for me the next afternoon, and we walked to the park together, to play. After the game he suggested that we sit under a tree and rest. I made quite sure we were two feet apart so nobody would talk about us.

"He began to get a little closer. I thought I would just

about die if somebody should see us. At that moment, a friend of my mother's happened to walk by. To this day I can live over how I felt."

"But Grandma! What difference could that possibly make?" asked Helen, completely mystified.

"Why, I thought she would tell my mother, and my mother would think I was doing something I ought not to be doing."

"Well, I must say you certainly lived in a funny time if things like that bothered you."

"But wait a minute," Grandma continued. "He asked me if he could write to me when he went off to college. I told him no, because I thought it wouldn't be proper to say yes at the very first, though I was just dying to have him write me so that I could show his letters to the girls.

"Well, we played another set of tennis, and then we went home, and he never asked again to write to me. Oh, how I suffered! Oh, how I wished I had only said yes! But he did write, after all, so all that agony was for nothing. He was probably suffering, too, thinking he shouldn't have asked to write to me. For just remember, boys can feel that they have made fools of themselves just as much as girls.

"Do you know what psychologists call that feeling? They call it the 'inferiority complex.' All of us, young and old, have it, and we have to fight it off. But somehow at your age it hurts the most. You feel that you are the only one who is always doing the wrong thing, saying what you shouldn't, that you are not popular, that everybody else looks better than you do and has a much better time at parties.

"In other words, you just feel sorry for yourself. You don't enjoy being that way the least little bit, but you can't seem to help it. At times you feel that you don't rate with the boys as much as the other girls do, and that makes you want to stay at home, away from the crowd, instead of being one of them."

"That's just exactly the way I feel, Grandma. What can I do to be popular?"

"First of all, remember this, and keep saying it over and over again to yourself. Every boy and girl in your class is feeling the same way, no matter how they act. Each one is putting on a bold front to hide how inferior he really feels. Do you realize that there are boys in your class who want you to like them ever so much, only they don't know how to go about getting you to like them? They feel that they say and do the wrong thing every time they are with you.

"It isn't going to be easy for you to follow my suggestion. But you just try this, the next time you are in a group of boys and girls. Pick out some boy that you know is awkward and self-conscious. Maybe he has pimples on his face and feels that he is ugly and unpopular. As you pass by him, make some comment that will make him feel good. You might say, 'My, I wish *I* could get the good grades in English that you do.' Or you might comment on how good-looking his necktie is, or make some equally trivial remark. But to him it would mean something tremendous that a girl as fine as you even noticed him.

"You wouldn't have to date him, or anything like that. But if you could make him feel comfortable for even a few minutes, that would be well worth while. If you just keep looking for things you can do or say to the boys and girls in school or camp who don't have your charm, you will soon find yourself forgetting your own troubles."

"But, Grandma, you *know* you don't think I have charm. Or do you, really?" asked Helen, in evident surprise.

"Why of course I do. You are one of the prettiest girls in camp, and everybody seems to like you."

"But most of the time I think nobody likes me," replied the girl, still not convinced.

"If you'll try my little trick of trying to make some of your friends feel more popular, you won't have to wonder whether you are popular or not. You won't be wondering whether you have on the prettiest dress, to make you attractive. You'll be sought after by boys and girls alike. Now dry your tears and run along, dear. Don't forget you are tops. Grandma is proud of you. Have fun these last days of camp."

The bugle sounded, and Helen ran off to the water front.

THE GIRLS ASK QUESTIONS

□ □ □ □ □ □ □ □ □ □ □ □

LADY AND DR. MARILYN JOHNSON WERE SEATED BY THE council fire as the girls filed down to their seats. Each dropped a question into a basket which had been placed on the ground. It seemed about to overflow. Unimportant and even silly as some of these questions might seem to people who did not understand girls, many of them concerned vital problems. Certainly, each deserved a thoughtful answer; and each would receive such treatment. The first to be picked out of the basket read as follows:

"I never seem to know what to talk about, when I am with a boy. I act so sort of stupid. Please tell me what to say."

Dr. Johnson turned with a smile to Lady, as if that were for her; and Lady began:

"Of course I don't know who asked this question. But whoever she is, I want to tell her first of all that she is far from stupid, else she would not be asking this very sensible question. She isn't alone in this. Lots and lots of girls are just like her in this particular.

"As for not being able to talk with a boy, because she can't think of anything to say, many an adult is just like her. Let me tell you the secret of success in conversation. Ask the boy one or two questions about himself, and then let *him* do the talking! You need hardly say a word; but look and act very much interested in what he is telling you. If he gets stuck, help him out a little bit by asking another question. Then do you know what he will say about you? 'I know one girl that I enjoy dating. She is so easy to talk to. She knows just what to say.' Try that little trick, and see how it works."

Another slip of paper: "My face is so covered with pimples I'm ashamed to go out anywhere. They make me look so ugly. Can I do anything to get cured?"

Dr. Johnson was most sympathetic with this questioner, for it happened that she had a daughter who was suffering from the same complaint. So she spoke with real feeling:

"I know exactly how you feel, and how you are suffering. But remember that there are many, many other girls, and boys, too, who are going through the same experience, at your age. For much of your trouble comes from the over-activity of the glands of the skin, that is one of the signs of commencing adulthood. Much of this trouble will disappear as you get older.

"But in the meantime, go to your doctor, and follow his directions carefully. They will differ according to whether your skin is over dry, or over oily. He will tell you exactly how to cleanse your face, and whether to use any medicine. Above all, he will instruct you about the use of make-up. Don't be tempted to try to cover up by using heavy make-up, which will clog the pores and make things worse. I'm sure he'll warn you against eating candy, and especially chocolate candy; and against sweet carbonated drinks.

"Never take the attitude that because your skin shows a few blemishes, you might as well give up, and not try to look your best. Bear in mind constantly that there is much more to being beautiful than having a pretty face. Your expression, the light that shines in your eyes, your sympathetic attitude, your thoughtful little ways, in fact your whole personality, will more than make up for any blemishes, in the eyes of the boy you are interested in, or of anyone else, for that matter.

"It often happens that a girl who suffers a little because of some such handicap, develops something within herself that is very appealing. Haven't you heard people say, 'O yes, she's pretty enough; but there's nothing there'? She has relied on that pretty face, and has not done anything to create real beauty. I would say to the girl who asked this question:

"Do all that you can to improve your complexion; and then forget it, to the best of your ability, and join in with your group in all of its activities. You will be amazed to find how few of them, whether boys or girls, notice what you think is the first thing they see. No, they want *you*, not your perfect complexion.

"This story illustrates my point. A girlhood friend of mine had very prominent ugly 'buck' teeth. She felt that everybody noticed these when she was introduced. She was so conscious of them that she was certain the boys would never go with her. But they did, and she married. Yet she had made a perfect bug-a-boo of those teeth; they still bothered her. The fact that her husband felt that she was foolish to worry about them didn't help at all. So she finally decided to do something about them.

"She went off on a so-called 'vacation,' and had something done to her teeth. I don't know just what the operation was; but somehow or other they were no longer prominent. She was delighted. How different life would be for her now!

"She came back, expecting everyone to comment on her

improved looks. To her utter amazement, nobody noticed the change! Nobody told her how much better she looked. 'Well,' she said to herself, 'if only I could have learned this lesson years ago, how much suffering I'd have been spared!'

"I suppose every one of you girls has something about you that you feel is a handicap. Some of you think you are too tall, others that they are too short. Some of you hate your hair and feel that there's nothing you can do about it. I know you must have noticed that I have a scar on my cheek, from an accident I had as a child. That used to worry me terribly, till after I had grown up I found that it made no difference to anybody but myself. All of us have something we don't like. Let's remedy it if we can, and then forget it and think of helping the other fellow."

The next question was for Lady: "*I* think it is all right for a girl to telephone a boy for a date. If the boys didn't like it, they would not make dates that way. I think they like to be invited by a girl, and have their way paid to a movie. What makes our mothers think they don't?"

The girls enjoyed this question immensely, and laughed merrily. Lady enjoyed it, too, though at first she did not seem quite sure what to say. After a moment's thought, she began:

"There's a lot of truth to what you say. I'll try to help you see your mothers' objections. We all know that social customs change with every generation. This is certainly true with boys and girls and dating. Your grandmother never went to a concert (there were no movies in her day) without a chaperone sitting beside her and her 'escort,' for that is what they used to call her date. And she had to be home by ten o'clock at night, too!

"She was told nothing about the physical workings of her body, or of the boy's. That was something she must never so much as hear mentioned. She must know nothing about such things before she married. She must be protected in every possible way. She was never permitted to be alone with a man; and so, her elders thought, nothing that was wrong could happen to her.

"Now your mothers had more freedom than that, but nothing like what you have today. Never, I suppose, has there been an age where there has been as much freedom and equality between boys and girls. It is a wonderful age for you girls to live in. But it means that a tremendous responsibility has been thrown on your shoulders. Your grandmothers never had any of it; and your mothers, only a little.

"You have to take your place in the world; but you must be fortified with every possible bit of knowledge about what folks used to call 'the facts of life.' For no chaperone will sit by your side at the movies, or ride with you in a car at night. It's up to you to know just how to conduct yourselves. It is possible that too much responsibility has been given you. I just don't know. But I *do* know that that is life today; and you must take it as you find it. This is just by way of introduction. Now let's get back to the question of the girl who's asking about telephoning a boy for a date.

"Yes, the girl who does that does get dates. And maybe some of the boys like it that way. But if you could ever hear the mothers of the boys you telephone to talk about those girls who are always calling up their sons and the comments the boys make about them, you'd see that lots of boys still like girls who aren't too forward, and eager to get them. I'll have to admit that many a boy has been caught by just those methods. But I don't believe it's the way that leads to the happiest courtship and marriage.

"I think the give and take between boys and girls today is

fine. It's a big step toward a better understanding. I believe it's a good thing for a group of teen-agers to go to the movies, and each pay for his own ticket. Otherwise you could not begin to have the fun together that you do. But if a boy wants to pay you a little courtesy because you are the girl, let him do it. There are those little things that do not cost him money at all, like being thoughtful and considerate and polite. Make it easy for him to be a gentleman. One day, when you are a little bit older, you will appreciate those little thoughtful ways. He has to learn; and you girls can help him."

Another piece of paper was drawn from the basket: "I'd like to ask a physical question. Should I go in swimming when I'm having my period?" Dr. Johnson answered at once:

"I believe the best medical authorities agree that it is best to stay out of very cold water at that time, even though you will see advertisements that say that you need make no difference in your daily life because of this. I also feel that there should be no horseback riding, or very strenuous exertion of any kind, like hiking or mountain climbing, especially for the first day or two. About other exercises such as tennis or golf, you can let your feelings be your guide. Individuals differ in this respect.

"Right here I'd like to put in a little word about refine. ment. There is so much freedom in the world today that we sometimes forget that we don't have to talk about a thing, just because we happen to know about it; and especially to the boys. You have been taught all about your physical development and that of the boys, and they have been told about you. They know that a girl has her periods, of course; but that is no reason why you should discuss the subject with them, as some girls have been known to do.

"Let's bring back a little of the refinement of other days,

without the ignorance that marked them. You girls want to attract boys who will appreciate those little touches of gentility. There are still the niceties of life, in this changing world of ours. And there are plenty of people of the better sort who look for them, and are glad when they see them, and are disappointed at their lack."

The next question made the girls sit up, and listen expectantly to Dr. Johnson's answer. It read:

"I once saw a sign that said 'Clinic for Social Diseases.' What did that mean? I asked one of the girls at school, and she said it was for bad people, folks who had done something wrong. But she didn't know, either. Can you tell us?"

"This is a question," Dr. Johnson replied slowly, "that I should like to avoid answering. But even if you hadn't asked it, I should have felt that I ought to bring up the subject. For you girls must know the facts, the bad as well as the good, if you are to be safe in this world.

"There are certain diseases that are known as the 'social diseases' because they are usually, although not always, the direct result of immoral association between men and women. You probably have heard that most states require a physical examination for a man and a woman who want to marry, so as to make sure that neither of them has a disease with which the other one might become infected.

"We'll have time for just one more question. Let's have the last one:"

"I always feel that everything I do is the wrong thing; and it makes me so unhappy. I say the wrong thing to boys; I say the wrong thing to my teachers. Then I wish I hadn't! What can I do about that?"

"Now, let me tell you something, whoever asked that question," said Lady, earnestly. "What you said to the boys, or to your teachers, probably wasn't the wrong thing at all. The fact that you think it was, doesn't make it so. Many girls are overly sensitive, at your age. It is a fine trait, in moderation, for it keeps you from hurting people's feelings. But you've gotten just a bit too sensitive, or critical of yourself.

"I know you girls get tired of hearing us older folks keep saying 'at your age this,' and 'at your age that.' But for these few years that you are living through right now, many things happen to you for just that reason. You do have feelings now 'at your age' that you won't have a little later. So be patient with yourselves, and don't let it worry you if you are hypersensitive about many things. And one of these is the thing you have just asked about; that is, thinking you have said or done the wrong thing, when you really haven't."

Dr. Marilyn Johnson and Lady rose together, and stood smiling their goodnight, while the girls broke up into groups, and walked away talking earnestly together.

THE LAST CAMPFIRE

□ □ □ □ □ □ □ □ □ □ □

LADY WAS LOOKING HER BEST. THE GIRLS ALWAYS
thought she was beautiful; but for the last campfire she
seemed to stand a little straighter, and her hair was fixed so
that it seemed just a little softer. She was lovely, as the light
from the fire lit up her face.

§

I never come to the last campfire of the season without a
lump in my throat; and I know each one of you girls is feeling the same way. But we are all going to swallow that lump.
There are to be no tears, either now or when you go to your
cabins. After all, this is just another day in camp; and after
we leave tomorrow, most of us will be seeing each other
all through the winter. And so we are going to be sensible—
at least for once in our lives!

I thought it would be fitting to run over a few of the things
we have talked about this summer, and get them clearly in
our minds. At the very beginning of camp we decided that
we would study ourselves, as we had never done before. We
would learn about ourselves, emotionally and physically, and
then see if we could not get along better with ourselves and
with other people.

We learned that we all go through a certain number of emotional stages. Each stage is important; and we take along with us through life some of the characteristics of each period of development. But there is always a danger that somewhere along the line between babyhood and womanhood we might stop, and stay too long at one stage. For example, it is natural for little girls to want to play only with little girls. But if at twenty-one there was no interest in wanting to be with men and desiring marriage, then they have been what psychologists call "fixated" at the little girl stage. You want to live to the fullest degree every stage of emotional development; so that when you are grown you can take your place in the world a mature woman, eager for the responsibilities of womanhood. If you know these things, you can help yourselves to grow up.

Dr. Marilyn Johnson has made perfectly clear to you the differences between boys and girls, and between men and women; why their bodies are alike in so many ways, and yet so very different.

We have had it very forcibly brought to us that all these new physical developments, that come at adolescence, bring new driving forces within us that are not always easily kept under control. Petting increases the physical desires, and so should be avoided. Only in marriage should there be any physical relationship between a boy and a girl, or a man and a woman. I know all my girls have made that decision already, for I know very well that each of you wants a happy home with children. You want the deep and lasting love of your husband.

Maybe Dr. Johnson and I have seemed a little cold and dictatorial about the girl and boy relationship in high school.

You may think that we have left the romantic age behind us so long ago that we forget what it is to have your heart beat fast when a certain boy looks at you. Some of you are going to feel before you leave school that you are old enough to love and be loved; and that you are at the perfect age for romance, else you would not be so stirred by moonlight, or a love song over the radio.

Not one of you girls here tonight can believe in love and romance more than I do. In fact, I might even say, *as much* as I do. I know what it means in reality; while so far you can only dream of it! There is nothing as important in life as love, the early love affairs, and those that mature later from friendships into a deep and lasting comradeship through life. Down through the ages poets have sung about love; and every great story is often great because of its love theme. This summer I have tried not to minimize love, but to emphasize it, so that you can begin to prepare yourselves right now for the great experience of romance that awaits you. You will not always find it easy, for nothing in life that is really worthwhile is easily won; but the goal is certainly worth striving for.

You have learned, I hope, this summer to understand your mothers better, to appreciate their efforts to help you, even if you feel that they are not always right. You have learned that in life there is a give and take of ideas, in order that we may live well together; and that talking things over is far better than becoming emotional, losing our tempers and saying things we'll wish we had not said.

Do you know that mothers, and fathers, too, for that matter, need not only to be understood by their daughters, but they need to be appreciated? You think so many lovely thoughts about them; but do you always tell it to them? Many of your parents have made real sacrifices this summer in order that you might enjoy camp and have a good time. Maybe they have done some nice little thing, like fixing up your room to surprise you on your return. Don't be afraid to let them know you like it. Oh, maybe it isn't just what you would have chosen; but keep that to yourself. For you do love the thought that made them do it. Mothers can stand an awful lot of loving.

I'll never forget when I was buying a pair of shoes for one of my daughters. There was one pair I could tell she wanted very much, but it cost two dollars more. She knew that economy in our family was very necessary, right then. But I couldn't resist giving her that pleasure, and so we bought the shoes. Never shall I forget the expression of absolute joy on her face, as she jumped up right there in the store and gave me a kiss! She was absolutely unconscious of anybody around her. I must confess it came as a surprise; but never have I spent two dollars that brought the returns that that did. In a way, it was such a little thing for her to do; but it was such a big thing to me. It will go with me through life. And so, give *your* mothers a little extra appreciation sometimes.

One of the biggest things that I hope that camp has given to you is friendships; friendships with each other, with the counselors, with Dr. Johnson, and with me. And I believe that all you girls will go back to school with a higher ideal of what a boy friend can be, and what you can be to that boy. Remember how many times I have said that your best times, at your age (here I go saying "your age" again) will be had in groups; boys and girls together in work and play. Then you will have learned to know many boys, so that when you are older you can have one special friend that will really mean something to you. Then will come the time when you should enjoy being with him, and him alone.

Now, I feel that I must prepare you for some of the disappointments that await you when you get back home. You are all so happy about going home; and that surely does my heart good. You have made up your minds not to let this or that bother you; but some of you won't be home many hours before you find yourselves all tangled up emotionally, and you will feel as if you could scream! Nothing will be going right.

You may have a little remorse when all is over; but that isn't going to help matters. Pick yourself up, give yourself a little shake, and say to yourself, "Of course I can't grow up all at once. Of course I shall make mistakes, and wish I hadn't; but I am going to try a little harder next time not to let having to wear a silly ugly old dress get me down. I will talk things over with mother; and I just know everything will be right again."

And the boys, oh the boys! They won't make you any too happy either, at times. One boy that was so nice to you before you went away doesn't notice you any more. You begin to feel sorry for yourself. Don't you forget now what I think about you, that you are just wonderful; and that in high school, *one* boy is not what you want anyhow. So look around and find another; and you may like him even better than the first!

About all your activities. You cannot be kept too busy. Join the school clubs, and work hard to make them succeed. Have fun at your parties, so that a parked automobile has little attraction. If you do that, you will get good grades at school, too. You have all dreamed your dreams this summer as to what you'll be some day; and I am counting on all those dreams coming true.

If I say anything more, I am afraid that lump will come back into my throat. So let's sing the camp song, and start packing. It's still early. The busses will leave camp promptly at nine tomorrow morning, and away you will go, laughing and singing. Be good now, and get to sleep early.

The girls broke up and walked off in groups. Mary Ann, Helen and Nell were arm-in-arm planning for the trip back tomorrow. Lady remained by the glowing embers until the last girl was out of sight. She lingered; and there was a prayer in her heart that each one would grow into womanhood fully equipped to make the world a better place, and to create a home that America could be proud of.

INDEX